Frank Lloyd Wright Prairie Houses

Frank Lloyd Wright Prairie Houses

PHOTOGRAPHS BY ALAN WEINTRAUB | TEXT BY ALAN HESS

with contributions by Kathryn Smith

RIZZOLI
NEW YORK

For Stephen and Cherye

— AW

For Debbie and Todd Herzer

— AH

First published in the
United States of America in 2006 by
RIZZOLI INTERNATIONAL PUBLICATIONS, INC.
300 Park Avenue South, New York, NY 10010
www.rizzoliusa.com

ISBN-10: 0-8478-2858-1
ISBN-13: 978-08478-2858-6
LCCN: 2006928780

© 2006 Rizzoli International Publications, Inc.

Photographs (except as noted throughout book)
© 2006 Alan Weintraub/Arcaid@arcaid.co.uk

Text (except as noted below)
© 2006 Alan Hess

"Frank Lloyd Wright Selected Plans" text (pp.
28–35) and "Exiles, Lovers, and Tourists: Florence,
1910" (pp. 268–271) © 2006 Kathryn Smith

Photography, drawings, and other artwork not
credited here are credited, as appropriate, in the
section in which such images appear.

Designed by Zand Gee Design

Printed and bound in China

2006 2007 2008 2009 2010/ 10 9 8 7 6 5 4 3 2 1

Jacket Cover: Arthur Heurtley House, Oak Park,
Illinois, 1902.

Jacket Back: Ferdinand and Emily Tomek House,
Riverside, Illinois, 1907.

Endpaper: Copper detail, Frederick C. Robie
House, Chicago, Illinois, 1908.

Page 4: Light detail, Frederick C. Robie House,
Chicago, Illinois, 1908.

Pages 6–7: Harvey P. Sutton House, McCook,
Nebraska, 1905.

Pages 26–27: Francis W. and Mary Little House I,
Peoria, Illinois, 1903.

Pages 36–37: Taliesin I, Spring Green, Wisconsin,
1911–1925.

Page 276: Stephen M. B. Hunt House II,
Oshkosh, Wisconsin, 1917.

Contents

Frank Lloyd Wright: The Prairie

By Alan Hess

Frank Lloyd Wright was a restless intellect. This temper goaded him throughout his astonishingly long and creative career; he had to be original, he had to be better than his competitors, he had to be better than himself. This posture first appeared in 1887 when the Wisconsin farm boy moved to the booming city of Chicago; a brief fifteen years later this questing spirit appeared full flower when he zeroed in on his first great architectural idea, the Prairie house. His ideas coalesced, his hand became confident, the forms gelled, and the clients came forward to produce a magnificent new expression of the house, America, and Modernism.

Over the next decade and a half Wright's intellect would flesh out a wide range of possibilities for this residential concept. Once his ideas were realized, he sought new and larger challenges to keep his intellect and his ego occupied. But in those fifteen years an array of fresh ideas took firm shape in over seventy houses that other architects would mine and ponder for generations.

Wright wove together brick, wood, and plaster to make intricate, remarkable spaces for his clients. Indoors and outdoors subtly merged, and a clever ornamental tracery of wood, lead, and glass unified them for the eye. Architecture learned to grow organically from its site and purpose; American families found new, more informal ways to live; and a growing suburban landscape found a confident and sophisticated expression.

Exploration and Discovery

In the last years of the nineteenth century, Wright made several discrete discoveries as he designed and built well over thirty houses in the Chicago area. For his own house, built in 1889, he embraced the era's popular new Shingle style, but also began breaking down the walls between specific rooms. While each room maintained it's separate identity, wide openings and open screens allowed the dining room to join the living room and entry. The dining room had its sideboard and great table for the important ritual of family and social dining; the living room had its relaxed fireplace and comfortable seating for conversation and music. In later houses, Wright refined this arrangement of spaces in an organic flow.

In the Winslow House (1893), he made a breakthrough with an imposing, singular roof tapering out into wide eaves. The boxy shape of the house (as seen from the street) was startlingly simple, even austere, compared to the reckless piles of towers and turrets of common Queen Anne houses of the era or the delicate Classical columns and pediments of the Colonial style. Instead, the house's planes of yellow brick glowed warmly, and the proportions of the wide front door (echoed by a broad stone border) made the house undeniably solid and comforting.

These proportions were odd for the times and had some of the exotic character of the Turkish Pavilion seen by visitors to the Columbian Exposition in the same year. In a fashion similar to that temporary building, Wright pulled the brick facing all the way up to the lower sill of the second floor windows, making the ground floor appear grand, and reduced the second floor to a narrow, dark band of shadowline that almost disappeared into the shade of the broad eaves. It was only an early example of the odd, unconventional and freakish designs that many critics and neighbors decried during his career.

For the Heller House (1896) on a residential city block lined with trees and sidewalks, Wright fashioned a three-story tower, as proudly vertical as the great highrises that his former employer, Louis Sullivan, had designed with Wright at his side. In the flat Chicago landscape, these houses and highrises were like great trees rising from and complementing the horizontal landscape. On Wright's path, this vertical design turned out to be an experiment that he ultimately rejected when he adopted the horizontal as the favored line for his Prairie houses.

From such experiments, Wright assessed what worked and what did not. The label of Prairie House came later, but the character of the Midwest where he grew up and launched his career shaped his thinking and designs. The land was flat, and so his rooflines responded by emphasizing flatness in their simplicity and shallow dimension. The land was open, and his houses spread leisurely out over their sites. It has often been remarked that none of his designs of this era were actually located on isolated prairie sites in the wide-open grasslands of the Central Plains. But most of Wright's designs were spacious in character nonetheless, and took advantage of the ample-sized suburban tracts developing on the fringes of the old center city. With forests, rivers or meadows, these sites were more akin to nature than the gridded, urban lots of central Chicago.

From these experiments grew the variety and beauty of the Prairie house. So rich was its language that other architects could use it to their own ends as well; Wright's ideas spawned one of the great movements in residential design. Over the following pages, in words and photographs, the range of Wright's imagination can be seen.

Willits House: Site and Space

Witness the many types of Prairie houses: the Willits House (1902) is assuredly symmetrical, while the Laura Gale House (1909) is an almost free-form composition of calculated asymmetries; the Heurtley House (1902) looks like a simple, contained box, while the Robie House (1908) suggests thrusting prows and decks of a transatlantic steamship; the walls of the Bogk House (1916) are solid, unpainted brick, while the walls of the Roberts House (1908) were plaster and glass in their original state; the Coonley House (1907) has the loose organization of a camp of tents, while the Darwin Martin House (1903) features a collection of pillars carefully arranged to subtly define its indoor and outdoor spaces. Each of these designs represents some of the individual, aesthetic ideas that Wright explored; all of the Prairie houses he built reflect one or another of these themes.

The large, flat lot on which the Ward Willits House sits is the suburban ideal: the free-standing structure sits in the midst of nature on a broad-clipped plain of grass surrounded by tall trees. The street meanders with the natural contour of a forest stream; no sidewalks impose the city's regularity and hard surfaces. The suburban illusion of pleasant solitude is guaranteed, even though the neighbors are well within sight. This is one of the natural habitats of the Prairie house, and of most of Wright's houses through his career.

This expansive setting allows the house to breathe. Its foundations stretch like tentacles beyond the walls into the yard, gathering in space, allowing the human habitat inside to link easily to the outdoors and nature. Typical of his Prairie designs, the house blurs the line between inside and outside by both setting it apart from and linking it to the ground. The entire house sits on a low platform of plinths and terrace walls that draw a clear distinction between nature and human construction. At the same time, these terraces self-consciously echo the expanse of nature itself, and are meant to easily draw the residents into the midst of nature. In later houses, Wright exaggerates this design tactic by extending long, low walls far out into the landscape, thereby claiming more land for habitation. Beginning with the Prairie houses, he placed ornamental urns at the extreme points of these terrace walls—like a ritual chalice raised in honor of nature, the gesture suited a nineteenth-century romantic like Wright.

The house itself sits as a great two-story pavilion in this greensward, with a lordly presence equal to any of the Colonial or Tudor houses in the neighborhood. Ever mindful of the social dimension of homes, Wright gave his houses a confident status to which his clients—usually well-established middle-class families active in the community—could relate. The house's plan itself is a cruciform. Wright carefully weighted the four wings to enunciate the visual and functional purpose of each. The powerful symmetry of the two-story central pavilion facing the street conveys the prominence and dignity of the house; it contains the living room on the first floor and the master bedroom on the second. The secondary wings on either side are set back to emphasize the central wing and to serve secondary functions for the porte cochere and entry on one side and an outdoor

Top to bottom:
Frank Lloyd Wright Home and Studio, Oak Park, Illinois, 1889; William H. Winslow House, River Forest, Illinois, 1893; Nathan G. Moore House, Oak Park, Illinois, 1895

Top to bottom:
William and Jessie M. Adams House, Chicago,
Illinois, 1900; Warren Hickox House, Kankakee,
Illinois, 1900; E. Arthur Davenport House, River
Forest, Illinois, 1901

Right:
B. Harley Bradley House, Kankakee, Illinois, 1900

terrace off the dining room on the other. The fourth wing, stretching to the rear, contains the kitchen and bedrooms.

Disciplined geometries of one sort or another continued to be Wright's preference through his career, but so were diversions from the symmetry in the service of function and expression. Here, the house's interior reflects the exterior's modified symmetry. With the entry hall and stairs on one side of the living room, and the dining room on the other, Wright contrived to subtly link these three spaces into a unified whole that retained the distinctive character and boundaries of each. Carefully placed screens of vertical wood accomplish these tasks by opening up views from one space to the next, while maintaining a certain degree of privacy. By using unpainted wood and brick inside, Wright further honored nature and weaved it into the architecture. The Willits House fully realized the themes of the Prairie house as a new statement of residential design: a fresh composition unattached to historic styles, an interior space reflecting a new, more relaxed lifestyle, and an embrace of nature.

Heurtley House: Form and Texture

Down the block from Wright's own 1889 home, the Heurtley House (1902) demonstrates a very different version of the Prairie themes. Wright's protean imagination never allowed him to be fully satisfied with repeating an idea he'd already worked out (though the business of running an office required him to); he felt more satisfied when he could engage with a new problem and offer a novel, fully realized solution.

In place of the Willits House's thin plaster skin outlined with wood trim, the Heurtley House has solid brick walls. But instead of leaving those walls as flat, featureless planes, Wright introduced a sumptuous, tapestry-like pattern that interweaved three colors of brick (not counting the stone coping) in a three-dimensional surface. Here, horizontal lines predominate. Although Wright did not return to this solution in later houses, he would repeat the theme of using materials rich in color and opulent in texture.

Built for family friends, the Heurtley House has a strong controlling geometry: the simple rectangular box. And once again, the design plays with the shifts, modifications, and re-arrangement of elements within this box. Unlike the straightforward, confident doorway in his clear-cut Winslow House just nine years earlier, the windows and doors of the Heurtley House are balanced asymmetrically. The design becomes an interlocking puzzle: the front door is hidden behind

Top to bottom:
J. J. Walser Jr. House, Chicago, Illinois, 1903;
Mary M. W. Adams House, Highland Park, Illinois,
1905; Charles A. Brown House, Evanston,
Illinois, 1905

Opposite:
Burton J. Westcott House, Springfield, Ohio, 1906

a low wall and the entry court is entered to the side, but a visible muscular archway—heralding back to his mentor Louis Sullivan and Henry Hobson Richardson—signals the door's presence. The simple platonic box is noticeably carved away, with a children's play yard on the first floor, a balcony terrace off the living room on the second floor, and a jutting prow off the second floor dining room. Windows are joined into bands so that they can play their role in the creation of this imposing façade—a public face that echoed the architect's growing self-confidence.

The living spaces of Prairie homes did not have to hug the earth. In the Heurtley House, as well as the Henderson, Tomek, and Robie houses, the main living rooms are raised to the second floor, like symbolic observatories for surveying the horizon. The Heurtley House's living and dining rooms flow together even more smoothly than they do at the Willits House, with glass doors creating a partition. Repeating the large brick arch at the front door below, the living room's hearth is an even more massive arch of brick set in a brick fireplace wall. In contrast to the intricate woodwork and leaded glass ornament surrounding it, this fireplace is a statement of the art and power of simplicity.

Dana House: Total Design

Frequently a client gave Wright the opportunity to design not only a house, but also the furniture, fabrics, windows, and furnishings as well. In 1902, Susan Lawrence Dana, a wealthy Springfield, Illinois, widow with progressive beliefs on suffrage and social work offered Wright such a commission. The brief: remodeling her existing Italianate home for herself and her widowed mother. In the end, the house was transformed.

Such a commission was the ideal for an Organic architect. A satisfying aesthetic unity

that relied on elaboration and complexity, rather than simplification and reductive uniformity, often resulted. Every element of the environment could be designed to relate to the others, geometric themes could be stated and repeated, and the complex geometry of the entire plan could be echoed in the smallest of ways, such as in the delicate tracery surrounding a light fixture.

Unlike the Willits House but like the Robie House, the Dana House was sited on a city lot in a residential neighborhood. Large enough for stables and gardens, its brick walls rose just a few yards from the sidewalks. Designed for entertaining, the large house included a library, art gallery, bowling alley, and a magnificent dining room. The Dana House's presence is notably different from most other Prairie houses. The front door is squarely visible on the sidewalk, and leads directly into a two-story reception area; large windows facing the street flood the space with light. Like the Winslow and Heurtley houses, the forms and proportions are different than the conventional Queen Anne or Tudor houses familiar to the public at the turn of the twentieth century: Wright's houses are self-conscious statements of the new.

The light tan brick of the ground floor rises high to the windowsills of the second floor. Just beneath the eaves, a strip of ornate tile separates the roof from the walls, giving the roof a sense of floating lightness that no Queen Anne roof, rooted in old-fashioned construction techniques, could approach. The pylons flanking the entry pavilion emphasize these unconventional proportions by giving the impression of a telescoping structure, rising from the solid foundation, then tapering to slender pillars to support the great roof. Experimenting again, Wright added an almost-Japanese fillip at the corners of the broad roof. With this unusual silhouette, the flattened gable form stands distinctly against the sky. Wright wanted the visitor to notice this roof, so he clad its fascia with a geometric pattern complementing the ornamental, leaded glass patterns found throughout the interior.

Wright would later often use two-story spaces (in the Isabel Roberts House, for example) to accentuate important rooms. Here, however, the two-story entry hall and dining room are more formal set-pieces than integrated, flowing spaces. He would rarely use the half-circle vault that tops the dining room again.

D. D. Martin House: Structure and Space

Where a continuous skin of plaster, wood and glass defines the Willits House's rectangular, wood-framed volumes, and where a solid brick block (with terraces carved out as contrasting negative forms) characterizes the Heurtley House, the Darwin Martin House (1903) takes the integration of structure and space a step further. Instead of a structure acting as a wrapping around the interior, the Martin structure of emphatic brick pylons and columns of various sizes merely suggests the lines between inside and out, of room to room. The columns are points in space that define various functions. The space itself takes on a much more palpable presence as it is arranged, even sculpted, by the architect.

The Martin façade shares the protruding two-story pavilion of the Willits' façade, but now it has been broken down into discrete elements directly expressing the structure itself. Wright made a nod toward a conventional solid corner by building up brick pylons in those positions, but then, counterintuitively, he cut the pylons off before they reached the roof; as capable of holding the roof as they appear, they are robbed of that function. The void at the second floor corner is filled instead with glass in a light wood frame, clearly unable

to carry the weight of the great roof. No matter; two other slender paired pylons, set well in from the corner, reach to the roof and support the cantilevered beams stretching out to the corners to carry the structure. With this architectural slight of hand Wright demonstrated the ability of modern construction to permit new expressions at once bold, dignified, and charmingly weightless.

This commanding façade of sturdy brick pylons and voids artfully telegraphs the actual structure of this house in the same way that Louis Sullivan's strong vertical pilasters on his early skyscrapers reveal the steel structure within, while expressively exulting in the art of height. To underscore this system in the Martin House, Wright

complemented the main pylons with secondary and smaller ones: two divide the first floor library window; the glass panes themselves are so deeply set that the brick structure dominates the façade. Low foundation walls act as outriggers, claiming the house's space on the property as an initial introduction to the main structure. Low pylons flanking the façade, are capped with Wright's trademark shallow, circular planter bowls held in a square rim. The central pavilion is, meanwhile, flanked by a large, two-story wing on one side, and a one-story veranda wing on the other.

The aesthetic is one of particulates. Wright broke down the structure into its functional elements, and then put them back together. This is interesting: what makes the

Top to bottom:
Thomas P. Hardy House, Racine, Wisconsin, 1905;
A. P. Johnson House, Delavan, Wisconsin, 1905;
Peter A. Beachy House, Oak Park, Illinois, 1906

Opposite:
K. C. DeRhodes House, South Bend, Indiana, 1906

Martin House great is that Wright applied the same concept to the plan of the rooms inside. The system of discrete brick columns and pylons introduced on the façade also defines the halls, corridors, rooms, and terraces of the living space. They are not truly rooms in the traditional sense of four walls containing a functional space; the system of thin brick columns and thicker brick pylons laid out along a tartan grid only suggest spaces, and one space easily flows, visually and physically, into another. The massive twin blocks of the fireplace divide the entry hall from the living room; six thin columns divide the living room from the veranda. The result is a unified composition where the space is the primary substance of the building, and the brilliantly conceived structure merely guides the sense of containment and the direction of that space.

The Martin House's composition obliterates the Beaux Arts and Colonial styles' reliance on symmetry for dignity and power. Though it echoes the asymmetrical composition of Tudor-style homes, it offers something different than the Tudor's picturesqueness. A sense of evolving time and eras gives that historic style's structure a patina of character and meaning. Wright offers the energetic balance of the new age—defined by railroads, telegraph, and airplanes—reflected in the precisely engineered structure and its artfully composed expression.

Cheney House: Hugging the Earth
Whereas most Prairie houses are two or three stories, Wright designed one that truly hugs the ground (even if it is truly two-stories tall). In the same way that the Laura Gale House tried out the themes seen in Fallingwater three decades later, the Cheney House created a modest and handsome prototype for the suburban ranch house in the second half of the century.

The main floor is virtually a square, and the low, gabled roof and brick chimney at its very center emphasize this shape. The design is simple and self-contained: Rooms are arranged symmetrically around the central axis, with the billiard room and living room on either side of the dining room and four bedrooms lining the rear of the house with views out to the back yard.

But the strength of the design is the simplicity of its roofline and volume. Wright's flourishes of stone plinth and coping atop the low brick walls show off craftsmanship and identify it as a solidly middle-class home. It is also, in Wrightian fashion, wedded to its site. As in the Willits House, a system of brick walls flank the property lines. The terrace, which continues the indoor space of the living room into the outdoors, also blurs the distinction between ground, foundation, terrace, and house. The house itself cannot be disconnected from this armature that ties it to the land.

Coonley House: Ornament and Space
No Wright house better illustrates Wright's use of integral ornament to strengthen the architecture than the Coonley House (1907). The large estate for a wealthy couple (each heir to family fortunes) sits on the banks of the Des Plaines River. The main house, the bedroom wing, and the dining wing, are all distinct, square pavilions distributed in a relaxed manner over the site. Bridges and corridors connect them into a rambling, spacious home. Together these wings create main and secondary courtyards that claim the outdoor space around the house, quite unlike the city-bound Robie House or even the suburban Heurtley House.

The front door is intentionally underplayed, as in many other Wright houses. Almost hidden under a second-story bridge connecting two of the several pavilions, the entry leads to a reception hall and stairs going up to a second-floor living room. A skylight floods these stairs with light, while a glimpse upward reveals the skylight's leaded glass artwork and a hint of the line and color to come in the living room. As much as any house of the period—and akin to the spaciousness of Wright's houses forty years later—the main living areas are one continuous space; Wright sculpted space even more than structure. The top of the stairs arrives at the corner of the broad, square living room. Above a strong cornice line, the ceiling rises in a concave pyramid, liberating the vertical dimension; a window wall on one side opens to the pool and garden, freeing the horizontal dimension. The room has, in effect, no corners, no boundaries. One corner flows into the broad hall of the stair landing, and stretches beyond that to the dining wing. With art glass windows letting in light, the wide corridor lined with bookcases and art is a space in itself.

Over this flowing spatial framework, Wright laid a system of continuous, fluid, wood trim that subdues corners and keeps the eye moving into the distance in one smooth movement. The ornament stops at appropriate points to emphasize a window, an intersection, or a doorway, but never stops its motion. Anchoring the entire system of ornament (as well as the space itself) is the fireplace. Broad and low, it repeats the sprawling motif seen throughout the design, in the estate's many pavilions, in the horizontal bands of windows, and in the long, wide eaves that punctuate each pavilion. The fireplace is framed by murals that artfully mirror the river and forest landscape surrounding the estate. Such unity is repeated in every Wright Prairie house, but for the Coonley House, with the client's ample budget and full support, Wright had every opportunity to fulfill his ideal design.

In his personal, professional, and aesthetic lives, Wright was adept at getting himself into trouble and often had difficult, contradictory ideals that ran against convention. He thrived under such conditions, skillfully resolving and integrating the complex principles that Organic architecture implied. The living room of the Coonley House is a case study in this skill: It merges structure, space, ornament, and furnishings, yet each element can be distinguished (and, what's more, enjoyed) and plays an essential role in the creation of a remarkable, indivisible whole.

Robie House: the Urban Prairie House

Critics and historians often note the irony of the decidedly urban site of Wright's definitive Prairie house, built for Frederick Robie in 1908. As Chicago developed fashionable neighborhoods near the South Side lakefront site of the 1893 Columbian Exposition at Jackson Park, new tracts were laid out in the usual city pattern of rectangular blocks, wide arteries, residential side streets, regular lots, and sidewalks. The neighborhood north of the long Midway Esplanade (site of the trailblazing amusement zone at the famous fair) stretching inland was home to several of Wright's clients.

Robie chose a prominent corner lot, but with a slightly awkward narrowness. Absent was the opportunity to create a bold object set off by greenery, as the Willits House's suburban lot permitted. The freedom of the Coonley's large estate was likewise

Top to bottom:
Frederick D. Nichols House, Flossmoor, Illinois,
1906; George M. Millard House, Highland Park,
Illinois, 1906; Raymond W. Evans House, Chicago,
Illinois, 1908

Opposite:
Meyer May House, Grand Rapids, Michigan, 1908

nonexistent. To achieve something remarkable here required Wright's skill. Fortunately, Frederick Robie was the kind of progressive thinker for whom Wright most enjoyed designing. A successful bicycle manufacturer, Robie detested the dark, cramped lifestyle of conventional houses of the day and wanted a house where his children could play outdoors, but where his family could also enjoy a sense of privacy.

Wright might have designed a house like the 1908 house for Edward Boynton, which also sat on a relatively narrow lot. There, the house becomes a dominant, rectangular block topped by a low-gabled roof and wide eaves; as counterpoint, a secondary cross axis provides extra floor space and opportunities to add light and terraces.

To best utilize the tight site, Wright created a three-story house for the Robies. That fact is striking, because the carefully crafted appearance is that of a long, low, ground-hugging structure. Where he had emphasized verticality dimension in earlier three-story houses with towerlike elements (see the Heller and Fricke houses), for Robie he completely subordinated the height to the long horizontal lines of the roof planes and the balcony railings that define the house. For extra measure, he continued these long lines out beyond the west side of the house into exaggerated cantilevered roofs sheltering the outdoor terraces and held in place by the same massive steel girders that Chicago shipyards used for their cranes and equipment—a useful up-to-the-minute technology that both Robie and Wright could appreciate. Thus Wright created a house with no relation to the usual volumes of traditional houses found in the neighborhood. It did indeed look like a great steamship (as many neighbors noted), a quality intentionally accentuated by the artful drawings and photographs Wright orchestrated in his presentations of this house.

The volume of the house is divided into two long, offset blocks. One is set along the back lot line for the service functions of the house, and the other stands, sleekly and perfectly proportioned, in full view of all passersby. The ground floor allows for a walled play area for Robie's children. The main public rooms are elevated to the second floor above the prying eyes of pedestrians on the nearby sidewalk; glass walls on each long side add to the rooms' airiness and views. Terraces run along the second floor so that the outdoors is only a few steps away. And the third floor, like the bridge of a ship, sits off-center as a balancing anchor to the unusual composition.

According to Wright's principles of Organic design, the solution for a building arises not from historic precedent, but from the character of the site, the client, and the structure. From these, the architect can derive a clean, practical, and beautiful solution that integrates each element.

Stockman House: Everyman's Prairie House

Custom home designs for affluent clients dominated Wright's Prairie work, as they did for all successful residential architects. Still he mulled over variations on the Prairie house that could bring an affordable, well-designed modern home to the middle class. He had pondered the impact of modern machines on architecture; the latest technology offered methods and materials that could be the key to providing solid, well-designed homes at a reasonable cost. As an architect devoted to the ethical and philosophical advantages of his ideas (and as an architect looking to widen his client base) the idea of an affordable, modern, efficient, and beautiful home was a problem he would return to throughout his seventy-year career. Such a house could be made of concrete, a material where the elements of the house could be easily and repetitively fabricated, reducing costs. At Unity Temple, Wright's design reflected its concrete structure: Rather than use concrete as a substitute for stone in an imitation of Gothic buttressing, he used the flat slabs naturally created by the forms for poured-in-place concrete to create a composition that expressed the building process itself. The same principle could be applied to a house. The plan could be regular (basically, a square) to simplify the structure and the building process; the interior plan could accommodate middle-class family life with open spaces, and middle-class aspirations with well-designed ornament and craftsmanship.

The ideas coalesced in Wright's design for a two-story, $5,000 fireproof house published in the popular *Ladies Home Journal* magazine in 1907. That house was never built in concrete, but Wright used its basic concept for several wood structure houses. For the Stockman House (1908) in Mason City, Iowa, Wright notably simplified the rich textures and spatial complexity of his other Prairie houses; it is essentially a self-contained cube, with two rudimentary wings for the entry and a porch. The four corners are each made up of solid slabs, suggesting structural pilasters. The cubic shape is emphasized ornamentally with strips of abstract wood trim, and the windows are neatly collected in centered bands on the first and second floors. Each side of the house is similar. Like other Prairie houses the eaves extend far past the walls.

Inside, the lavish woodwork found at the Coonley House is edited down to the essential lines. Still, this ornament also unifies the horizontal space of the public rooms, which flow into each other around the central chimney block. A trim board runs around the entire space a foot below the

ceiling, lowering the center of gravity of the room and directing the eye. The fireplace is a simple brick plane with a flat inset mantel, but here the simplicity of the fireplace is not contrasted with the elaboration of the room around it. Even the leaded glass windows are reduced to a simple motif of three horizontal lines divided by a single vertical one.

Wright drew on this straightforward design a few years later for his first real effort at mass produced housing, the American System-Built homes for developer Arthur Richards. They were also made of wood and covered in stucco rather than the daringly modern concrete he first envisioned. However, in later years, he lost interest in the slab forms of monolithic concrete

construction and experimented instead with concrete block in his California houses in the early 1920s and the Usonian Automatic houses in the 1950s.

Laura R. Gale House: Prairie Free Form

In certain ways, the Laura R. Gale House (1909), is a residential version of Wright's Unity Temple (1904), also in Oak Park. This house is very different, in terms of composition and form, from the other Prairie houses, and even further from conventional domestic imagery of peaked roofs and shuttered windows. It has flat roofs where other Prairie houses have sweeping gabled roofs. It is vigorously asymmetrical where other Prairie designs are only subtly asymmetrical. However, the bands of

terrace, one atop the other, emphasizes the manner in which the structure vividly captures and defines space, without the need for traditional enclosure. It expresses a modernistic daring that would not reappear in Wright's buildings until 1936 with his dynamic Fallingwater home in eastern Pennsylvania. But for thirty years before that, the Gale House stood as a striking example of a house that did not look like a house. As late as 1954, historian and designer T. H. Robsjohn-Gibbings used the 1909 Gale House as his emblem of the modernist statements of Wright in his survey of modern styles, *Homes of the Brave*.

Taliesin: Wright's Prairie Home

Though he kept building Prairie houses as commissions rolled in after 1910, Wright's tumultuous personal life and travels to Europe and Japan reduced his day-to-day involvement with his office. Often his talented present and former employees (including Marion Mahony, Francis Barry Byrne, Walter Burley Griffin, William Drummond, and others) oversaw, finished, or undertook these projects. Each was skilled and committed to the Prairie architecture themes of structural expression, connections to nature, and open interior plans.

One project, however, re-ignited Wright's imagination: a house for himself and his mistress, Mamah Cheney, in his childhood hometown of Spring Green, Wisconsin. He named it Taliesin, a Welsh name reflecting his family heritage and the personal nature of the house.

The 1911 project had more than enough ingredients to challenge his imagination. The site was among the most dramatic for which he had ever designed. Instead of narrow city blocks or even expansive urban lawns, this was the countryside. The site was a hill overlooking a small lake, rich with natural beauty and personal memories; he had

windows, organic woodwork, and startling forms still link it to the other Prairie houses.

The Gale House explodes outward from its center: thick, horizontal planes thrust out in two directions, complemented by the thinner planes of the flat roof. Sizable vertical pylons thrust upward through these planes in a carefully considered arrangement that gives the design a kinetic stability along with its thrusting energy. Some of these vertical planes shoot up to the level of the second story windows, where they end as planter boxes for weeping vines; others rise above the roofline as the chimney mass.

The radical forms still accommodate a suitable middle-class residence; Mrs. Gale lived in the house until 1943, and the house remained in the family for several decades after that. Inside, the arrangement of rooms is slightly adjusted from more common, carefully balanced Prairie houses such as the Willits House. The Gale fireplace is placed off-center in the living room, and the extra space allows the dining room beyond to join in a single continuous living area.

It is the cantilevered second floor balcony, paired with the terrace off the living room below it, which gives the Gale House its distinctive and even prophetic look, compared to other Prairie designs. The repetitive, cantilevered forms of the roof fascia, second floor balcony, and living room worked hard as a farm hand on his uncle's farms nearby as a youth. As his own client, he could push ideas and experiment with forms freely, just as he had in his 1889 home in Oak Park. More than a home, Taliesin was an entire farm estate, and the barns for animals and gardens for vegetables added another new dimension to the design. Taking a cue from the shape of the hill, he placed the house on its edge and allowed it to circle in a leisurely manner along its edge. One room led to the next in a rambling U-shape, more casually than the extensive Darwin Martin or Coonley estates. The structure stepped slowly up the hill to a high point where the structure leaped upward in a viewing tower. Nothing needed to be constricted or contained. For materials, Wright quarried a local stone, giving the house a more rugged, ancient, settled appearance than any of his other houses up to that time. In a manner he would repeat in the future, these materials made the house appear to grow out of the earth.

Taliesin was still a Prairie design, however. Its collection of broad gabled roofs and wide eaves hovered over the land. Pillars and pylons defined the structure and the spaces. A system of landscape elements— auto gateway, open entry loggia, low walls, planters, steps, and terraces—matched the stone walls of the house and tied them all together into an organic whole. Inside, broad bands of windows stretched along rooms to bring in light and the tranquil views. Wood trim ornamented and unified the plaster walls inside. As another harbinger of his future directions, the geometry of the house loosened up. Though still intricately choreographed with a mix of low, intimate spaces contrasting with large, dramatic spaces, this plan was freer in form. Some of the fussiness of the woodwork, a holdover from the Victorian era, was relaxed.

Like his Oak Park home, Taliesin was a laboratory for design and would change over the years. Like his Oak Park home, those changes often resulted from highly personal events and tragedies. Major portions of it burned over the years, only to be rebuilt. As much as any Wright building, it is his architectural autobiography.

Ravine Bluffs: the Prairie Neighborhood

For all his obvious delight in designing sumptuous individual commissions with matching budgets, Wright's intellect continued to contemplate larger planning and architectural issues. He may have held the general level of urban planning in disdain, but he often considered his designs as pieces of an entire neighborhood, or a whole city. The $5,000 fireproof house offered a solution for a house that could be repeated over and over; he also began to think in terms of groupings of houses—a theme that he would return to thirty years later in developing his concept of Broadacre City.

But for a start, he thought on the scale of a single tract of suburban homes. He did design and build a handful of urban apartment houses, but Wright is more truthfully seen as the first great architect of suburbia, of the fringes of the center city which began to develop on a large scale in American cities in the late-nineteenth century as trolley cars made open space beyond the city limits accessible to home buyers—and therefore of interest to building developers. Wright had designed several of the homes on Oak Park's Forest Avenue (including his own house) but they were not designed together, and varied from the Tudor-style Moore House to the Prairie-style Thomas House. Today, they constitute a remarkable if diverse collection of Wright designs. In 1913, however, Wright conceptualized an arrangement of houses in sets of four, where shared landscaping and clustered structures would leave more open

Top to bottom:
Eugene Gilmore House, Madison, Wisconsin, 1908; Hiram Baldwin House, Kenilworth, Illinois, 1909; Jessie R. Ziegler House, Frankfort, Kentucky, 1910

Opposite:
Laura R. Gale House, Oak Park, Illinois, 1909

Top to bottom:
O. B. Balch House, Oak Park, Illinois, 1911; William B. Greene House, Aurora, Illinois, 1912; Edmund F. Brigham House, Glencoe, Illinois, 1915

Right:
J. Kibben Ingalls House, River Forest, Illinois, 1909

space and a more cohesive streetscape. A single house design with four distinct facades could be shifted on the lot to create variation. The closest he came to building an entire planned neighborhood at one time, however, was the 1915 Ravine Bluffs development in suburban Glencoe, Illinois. The owner of the property, Sherman Booth, was Wright's lawyer and had commissioned his own house; he also asked Wright to design several other houses for rental properties.

Unlike Forest Avenue, Sylvan Road and Meadow Road are picturesquely winding suburban streets. No sidewalks hem in the grassy lawns. The curving drive causes the Wright-designed houses to present ever-changing views as cars motor by, a perspective which emphasizes the three-dimensional sculptural compositions of Wright's evolving design work; the overhanging roofs, vertical fireplaces and asymmetrical facades change and shift against the backdrop of trees as the visitor moves around and past each house.

The six houses he designed for Ravine Bluffs are recognizably in the Prairie style, but Wright did not himself supervise their construction. By 1915, Wright's life and career had altered dramatically. In 1909, he abruptly left his wife and family to spend a year in Europe with his mistress, Mamah Cheney. Returning to Chicago, he made plans to build Taliesin in his native Spring Green, Wisconsin, away from a society that disapproved of his chosen lifestyle. He hoped to continue his career, of course, and large commissions came his way, including Midway Gardens in Chicago in 1913 and the Imperial Hotel in Tokyo in 1915. By this time the ideas of the Prairie house no longer held his attention; though the planning ideas of the Ravine Bluffs project was interesting, the houses were not as inspired or inventive as the series of distinct and varied interpretations he had regularly produced throughout the first decade of the century.

New ideas continued to pour from his imagination, but as in his explorations of the 1890s, they were slow to coalesce into a cohesive approach to residential design. The pivotal design for his leap into a new expression seems to have been the home he designed—over several years—for Aline Barnsdall, an oil heiress he met in Chicago who soon relocated to Los Angeles. In 1916, Wright's initial designs for her house were Prairie in style. By the time the design became Hollyhock House, the horizontal roofs and terraces of Prairie design evolved into massive, Mayan-temple-like forms of battered walls. The openness of a Prairie house's glass walls and ribbon windows had turned into solid planes with a few deeply recessed openings.

Top to bottom:
Lewis E. Burleigh House, American System-Built Homes, Wilmette, Illinois, 1915; Arthur R. Munkwitz Duplex Apartments, American System Ready-Cut, Milwaukee, Wisconsin 1916; Emil Bach House, Chicago, Illinois, 1915; Opposite: Henry J. Allen House, Wichita, Kansas, 1916;

Page 24: Frederick C. Bogk House, Milwaukee, Wisconsin, 1916

Boynton and Bogk Houses: Moving On

The shifts in Wright's aesthetic path at the end of the Prairie years—capturing an ideal, losing interest in it, and beginning to move in other directions—can be seen by comparing two designs, the Boynton House (1908) and the Bogk House (1916).

Even with the considerable range of forms and compositions within Prairie design, the Boynton House is a solid example of its innovations. A custom design for a man of resources, this Buffalo, New York, house is a boldly abstract modern volume. A long, rectangular box defines the main axis of the exterior; a secondary axis provides a counterpoint to the composition. White plaster covers the houses, with contrasting wood trim drawing attention to the horizontal masses instead of the vertical.

In many neighborhoods, Prairie houses stand next to Queen Anne or Colonial houses. The contrast is always striking and can still convey, even today, the dramatically strange character of Prairie houses in their day. One woman who hired a Wright competitor, Howard Shaw, to design her 1914 house criticized Wright's houses as looking like gas stations; it was not the last time that verdict would be reached. So new were their concepts that there was little else with which to compare them. For many of Wright's clients, of course, this was a positive advantage.

The Queen Anne style was vertical, with a mélange of towers, turrets, steep roofs, and dormers borrowed, roughly, from the appearance of European chateaux and manor houses. The Colonial style (a decent example stood next door to the Boynton home) turned a square, two-dimensional face to the street. Its static composition was emphasized by the chaste symmetry of its ornamental quoins, columns, pediments, and Palladian windows. Representing the Prairie style in contrast, the Boynton House

carefully composed its distinguishing forms as a deeply modeled sculpture: the deep shadows of the wide eaves, the solid pillars anchoring the corners, the dark voids of the windows gathered in horizontal ribbons. To virtually force the visitor to approach the house at an angle where it is best seen (and understood) as a three-dimensional form, Wright placed the door halfway down the side of the house, off the side drive.

Whereas traditional architectural styles maintained a dignified separation from the surrounding effusion of nature, Wright's houses built prominent planters into the very design of the house—a firm statement of his belief in nature. Whereas the Colonial style displayed its traditional ornament in full view for all middle-class people to understand and admire as an expression of the inhabitants' status, Wright self-consciously reinvented most of the house's elements to be new, unconventional, and following their own logic.

Inside, Wright pushed out the Boynton's dining room wall to enlarge the space in a nook with a lower ceiling. The taller ceiling in the dining room allowed light to flood in through clerestory windows—complemented by glass and wood lighting fixtures. Wright emphasized the asymmetry of this room's natural and artificial light, and of its varied ceiling heights, in the exquisitely delineated ornamental detail: The band of upright clerestories along one side are complemented by the recessed lighting fixtures that are linked to the opposite wall with strips of wood running on the surface of the plaster. The safe, formal balance of Colonial design had been replaced with a strikingly dynamic balance. Even the dining table (designed by Wright) incorporated four lights into its four legs as they rose above the tabletop.

To see how far Wright had moved from this Prairie ideal eight years later, note how the Bogk House (1916) breaks many of the

Boynton House's conventions. It is still arguably a Prairie house: the strong corner piers reflect the Stockman House, the integral foundation planters echo the Willits House, the wide eaves repeat the Boynton House, and the natural brick mirrors the Darwin Martin House. But the design is more self-contained. The protrusions are less dramatic, the house is pulling into itself. The windows are strikingly different too; instead of the bold bands and window walls that burst out beyond the walls (as in the Roberts House living room), these windows are deep set voids. Along the side drive, they disappear into tall slits that rise two stories to the eaves.

The interior plan reflects the design's self-containment. Other Prairie houses allow the main living spaces to flow around the central mass of the chimney. Here, however, the space is more literally a continuous spiral of space around the central fireplace mass. Natural light is evenly distributed, but the large expanses of view windows are absent.

Perhaps the most notable difference between the Boynton and the Bogk houses is the use of ornament. At the Bogk House, sculptural, cast stonework forms a frieze at the top of the street façade and around the main windows. Wright had not used such

prefabricated one- and two-story houses, and apartments, which also used the Prairie style, though they were modified for simplicity of construction. But the years of exploration of the Prairie themes were over. Wright was moving on.

The End of Chapter One
Houses that responded to their natural setting rather than centuries of architectural tradition; houses that treated space as a material to be shaped; houses that used the rough texture of hewn stone, the regular rhythm of brick, the warm tones of wood for their tactile appeal; houses that blended one room into the next to express a new, American, suburban lifestyle: these themes of Organic architecture, drawn together by the thirty-three-year-old Wright in 1901 would serve him for a lifetime. But they would take forms different than those of the Prairie houses.

For a decade Wright massaged these themes, giving them a remarkable and vivid variety of forms. Can the Robie House, with its long terraces and long roofs hovering over space, and the Heurtley House, with its single, emphatic roof like a cap on a box, both be labeled as Prairie houses? Consistency obviously did not concern Wright, though unity did. These houses show the way a great architect takes a rich, complex, evocative idea and gives it new, fresh form, over and over, in shrewd response to new conditions.

But after that first decade or so of work, he had played out those ideas. After the Prairie years centered in the Midwest (he built one example in California, and none on the East Coast) he cast around for new ideas to engage him. He hoped to trade up, designing larger buildings, and the Midway Gardens in Chicago and the Imperial Hotel in Tokyo seemed to promise such a future of opulent color, texture, and ornament. But

modeled, sculpted surfaces since the 1890s when he was still influenced by the ornamental flourishes of Louis Sullivan; now he made this ornament even more emphatic, and explored its possibilities in the Midway Gardens, Imperial Hotel, and German Warehouse designs. The Bogk House points ahead six years to the concrete-block houses of Los Angeles. There the modeled surface flows over the entire house, creating a solid, massive volume of masonry far

different than the light balloon frames and thin plaster surfaces of most Prairie houses. With window openings as deep set and often as thin as those of the Bogk House, the Los Angeles houses also retreat defensively into themselves.

Along with the Henry Allen House in Wichita, Kansas, the Bogk House is among the very last Prairie houses by Frank Lloyd Wright. He did design several prototypes for the Richards American System-Built

after the Imperial Hotel opened in 1922 his career faltered. Surprisingly, the excess and prosperity of the Jazz Age that gave birth to the Art Moderne style did not produce a sufficient flow of clients to keep Wright busy.

When he revived his career in the mid-1930s, the startling and fresh shapes that captivated the architectural world still echoed the themes of the Prairie designs. By then Wright had grown and matured as an artist. The times had changed as well, and though he often positioned himself in the avant garde, leading culture into a brave new world, he was also sensitive to real social changes. The new manners of family life without servants lead him to bring the kitchen out of the service wing (where it was usually placed in the Prairie houses) and integrate it into the dining and living areas. The public's expanding reliance on the automobile caused him to refine his suburban residential designs; he placed the car and its carport in a prominent place in each design. The porte cochere—often an integral part of a Prairie house composition—evolved into the open carport of the Usonian houses in the last decades of his designs.

As an artist, Wright's forms became more fluid and generous. Prairie houses had regular, neat surfaces of plaster or neatly laid brick; in later houses he became more enamored with the beauty of raw earthen materials. The dressed, limestone walls that gave Taliesin in Spring Green a pleasingly weathered, timeworn look evolved in later years into even, rugged walls of uncut desert stones left exactly as they had been hauled from the desert floor by his apprentices. Carefully selected for color and texture but otherwise completely natural, they were set in a rough matrix of concrete.

Wright's interest in strong geometry continued in his later career, but also evolved. Instead of the complex but strictly ordered tartan grids of many Prairie designs,

he explored the effects of honeycombs, triangles, and oblique angles. As an artist, Wright became less reticent and more confident in large, singular gestures and lines, though always expressing a rich opulence rather than the reductive, minimal abstractions seen in the work of his International Style nemeses. The 1942 design for the Guggenheim Museum in New York is the archetypal example: It is but a single line, twisted into a spiral that is always changing to the eye.

In the Prairie years, a great roof almost always had been a major element of the design, and that sheltering image of home and hearth echoed again and again in his later work. His later roofs took on new expressions, however: the Buehler and Elam houses took the roof and swept it upwards in a dramatic form that influenced a generation of architects after 1940. In the Walker and Gillin houses, low octagonal domelike roof forms dominated the designs.

Minor themes of the Prairie years became major themes in his later years. Most Prairie houses had a dominant symmetry, such as the two-story pavilions of the Willits and Roberts houses. Look closely at those house plans, however, and you will observe a subtle asymmetry in the placement of elements within; for example, a wing with an open porch on one side balances a wing with an enclosed dining room on the other.

In his later career, the emphasis reversed: the houses had a dominant asymmetry. Many houses were carefully worked out compositions of long, horizontal decks balanced by solid, vertical chimney towers, of carport voids balanced by solid brick walls. The same reversal came in Wright's use of diagonals. In the Prairie years, a few houses had minor window bays that jutted out from the rectilinear house at a forty-five-degree angle. These small counterpoints added

energy to the design by breaking the governing geometry. This changed dramatically in his design for his own 1938 home in Scottsdale, Arizona, where broad diagonal lines are the main organizing framework for the structure, with secondary rectilinear lines playing off of them.

Similarly Wright's use of circles changed radically over the years. In the Prairie years the circle was an occasional decorative punctuation; at the Robie House, a series of globe lights are held delicately in an angular frame within an angular living room. He dropped circular planter bowls throughout his Prairie houses, usually perched as punctuation on the end of garden walls, but each is contained in a square rim. From the 1920s onward, however, the curve became a larger presence and a favored motif in his work: at Hollyhock, a circle encloses a terrace like a broad arm; in the Ralph Jester project, each room is a circle; the Guggenheim Museum, of course, is a spiral.

Circles, diagonals, asymmetrical balance—Wright introduced each into his design vocabulary during the Prairie years, and in them he discovered, even after the Prairie style itself was exhausted, new avenues for his imagination. They were among the fertile seeds he nurtured to reinvent himself and his architecture—and, it can be argued, Modern architecture itself. Also in the Prairie years, Wright first encountered his own limits, his ability to exhaust his imagination along certain lines as he became bored with Oak Park, family life, and the Prairie style. It matured him; though he often struggled professionally in later years, he invented ways to keep himself fresh and stimulated in his art. As he matured he discovered in his vocabulary of forms and his forceful persona a broad, gestural simplicity that suited his confident hand—and Wright was nothing if not confident, as a man and as an architect. •

Frank Lloyd Wright Selected Plans

By Kathryn Smith

At the beginning of the twentieth century, Frank Lloyd Wright initiated the first revolution in architectural space since the Renaissance. He chose the American middle class family home as his subject and the plan, rather than the perspective, as his means. For Wright, the plan was the generator of form. Although Prairie houses displayed tremendous variety in their materials, sizes, and even their building programs—from lakeshore cabins to commodious residences to grand estates—there was a consistent design process in the composition of the plan. In the period between 1892 and 1900, Wright developed a rationalist methodology. By analyzing the functional components of the single family dwelling, he went from what he called "the general to the particular." For instance, he established a hierarchy with the public spaces (living room, dining room, library) as primary and the service spaces (the entry, kitchen, pantry, servant's rooms) as secondary. Using orthogonal planning and a square grid as ordering devices, he gave geometric expression to the hierarchy of spaces in plan. With these devices, he applied a new sense of abstraction that was distinctly modern in sensibility.

A major conceptual breakthrough was the realization that mechanized heating made it no longer necessary to close rooms off from each other to conserve heat. This discovery led to the open plan in public spaces while maintaining compartmentalized rooms for services. With the hearth no longer used as the major source of heat, Wright was free to liberate it from the wall and use it as a freestanding vertical plane in space. By treating the fireplace as a solid screen that defined but did not enclose space, he created the open plan of modern architecture.

In 1900, the results of this process of analysis and synthesis produced the two major Prairie house plan types—the in-line plan seen in the Warren Hickox House (1900) and the cruciform plan as developed in the B. Harley Bradley House (1900). From these two examples, the majority of the Prairie houses were generated for the next decade. The in-line plan opened the major living spaces along a cross-axis with the fireplace in a central position placed frontally. The services were aligned at the rear and often deflected from the primary forms as the client's requirements and space dictated. The T-plan developed with the living room extended forward to provide light on three sides and the services deposed to the rear along a primary axis. The fireplace acted as a pivot point with each of the four wings rotating around the solid core. The open corner where the living room joined the dining room established a strong visual diagonal axis that added increased spatial dynamics to the plan. From these two plans, endless combinations were produced such as the L-shaped plan, the in-line plan of two sliding volumes, and the zoned-courtyard plan with bedroom and service wings added as appendages.

The generous suburban plots of Oak Park, Riverside, Wilmette, and Highland Park allowed Wright to extend the building out into the landscape. Transitional spaces between indoors and out-of-doors such as terraces off the living room or an open porch adjacent to the dining room opened the interiors to light and views. In the hierarchy of spaces, the entry was relegated to a minor position so it was often necessary to stroll around the perimeter of the house (as in a Japanese stroll garden) affording revealing perspectives of the structure from various angles before arriving at the front door.

Selected Plans:

1. Warren Hickox House (1900)
2. Edwin H. Cheney House (1903)
3. Frederick C. Robie House (1908)
4. Laura R. Gale House (1909)
5. Ward Willits House (1902)
6. Frank W. Thomas House (1901)
7. Darwin D. Martin House (1903)
8. G. C. Stockman House (1908)
9. Avery and Queene Coonley House (1907)
10. Taliesin I (1911)
11. Frank Lloyd Wright Studio (1897)
12. Unity Temple (1906)

Warren Hickox House (1900)

The in-line plan established the main living areas (living room, dining room, music room or library) as one continuous open space aligned along a secondary axis. The service spaces were deposed at the rear deflected to accommodate needs. This plan type was subject to great spatial flexibility as the fireplace is treated as a freestanding vertical plane. Most typically (as in this example), it was placed frontally on the primary axis. However, Wright felt free to shift its position to create variations. This plan type reappeared in the F. B. Henderson, Burton Westcott, Edwin Cheney, Charles Brown, Ferdinand Tomek, and Frederick C. Robie houses.

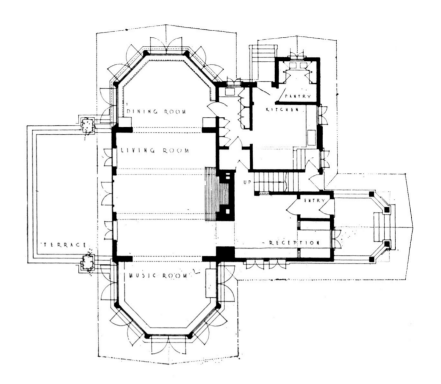

Mamah Borthwick and Edwin H. Cheney House (1903)

The in-line plan set within the square volume of a block. The hearth is on the primary axis and the central focus of the plan with the generous public rooms facing the street and bedrooms lined up behind the central hall. The services (kitchen and entry) are tucked into either side of the fireplace. The high degree of symmetry will disappear in later Prairie houses.

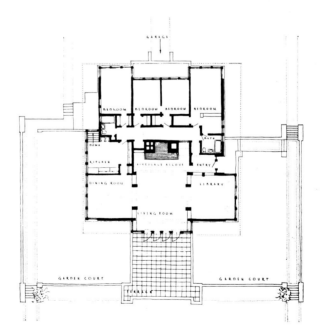

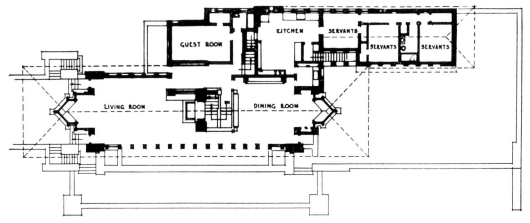

UPPER FLOOR

Frederick C. Robie House (1908)

The plan for the Robie House is the most sophisticated version of the in-line plan that had its origins in the Robert G. Emmond House (1892). In this example, the fireplace used as a freestanding vertical screen has been shifted on line with the primary axis, serving as a spatial divider between the living room and dining room. The over-all organization consists of two side-by-side rectangular volumes (an expression of the hierarchy of primary and secondary spaces) with the service wing slid off the cross-axis. Wright also used the additional device of a piano nobile or raised living floor to afford better views.

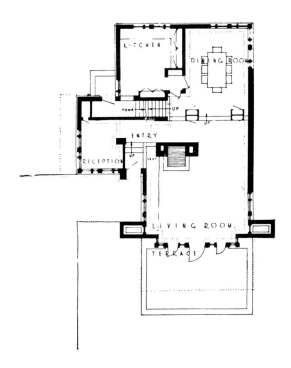

Laura R. Gale House (1909)

This example exhibits Wright's complete mastery of the in-line plan type and his ability to use the square grid to shift elements while maintaining clarity and order. While the living room and dining room are on-line, the fireplace has been rotated ninety degrees and shifted off axis. The services have shrunk to a compact kitchen and placed side-by-side with the dining room. The entry-reception is appended outside the main rectangular volume of the building. The terrace acts as a transition zone to the out-of-doors.

Ward Willits House (1902)

The classic cruciform plan, which had been published as "A Small House with 'Lots of Room in It'" in the *Ladies' Home Journal* (July 1901), raised the type to the level of abstract clarity. The space is centrifugal, radiating around the fireplace core. Strong diagonal axes are established from the entry into the living room and between the living room and dining room. This plan reappears with variations as the E. Arthur Davenport, Francis Little (1902), Charles Ross, J. J. Walser Jr., Darwin D. Martin, George Barton, William Heath, A.W. Gridley, K. C. DeRhodes, L. K. Horner, and Isabel Roberts Houses.

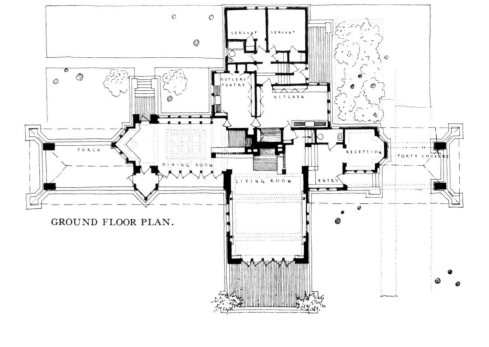

GROUND FLOOR PLAN.

Frank W. Thomas House (1901)

The cruciform truncated into an L by retaining the diagonal relationship of the two public rooms (living room/library and dining room); but reducing and compacting the service space (entry and kitchen). The use of the square grid allows Wright to subtly shift elements off axis creating syncopated relationships, especially between indoors and outdoors (as in this example between the living room and verandah).

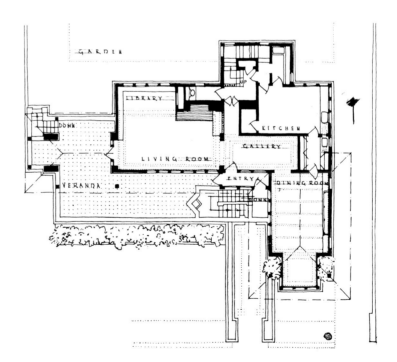

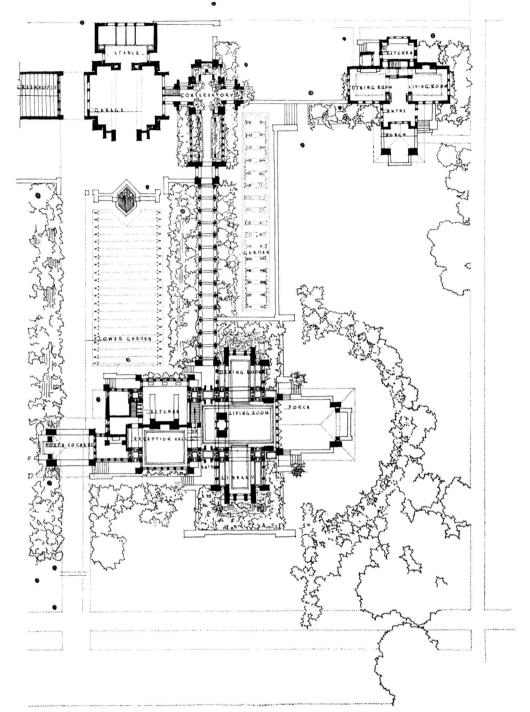

Darwin D. Martin House (1903)
The cruciform plan is used as a theme for an elaborate grand estate encompassing a main house, secondary house, conservatory, and garage. Within the main house, the spaces are defined by the strict symmetry of the primary rooms (living, dining, library) and the asymmetry of the service wing (reception hall and kitchen). The vocabulary of the square grid is pronounced with the articulation of eight pier clusters at the corners of each room.

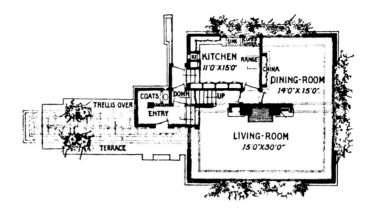

G. C. Stockman House (1908)

Originally published as "A Fireproof House for $5000" in *Ladies' Home Journal* (April 1907), this plan type reverted to the foursquare organization of the 1890s subjected to geometric abstraction. With primary and secondary axes crossing to create four quadrants, Wright allocated the spaces hierarchically (living room equaled two quadrants, dining and kitchen one each). The entry was added as an appendage. This primary form was subject to clients' demands so that spaces were deflected outside the square as appendages or wings to suit the program. Variations include Frederick Nichols, P. D. Hoyt, Andrew Porter (Tanyderi), Stephen Hunt, and Raymond Evans.

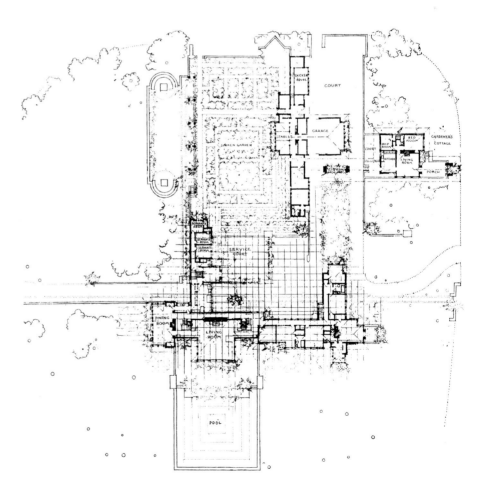

Avery and Queene Coonley House (1907)

The cruciform plan reconceived on a large scale, zoned hierarchically into public rooms (living and dining), bedrooms, and service (kitchen and servants). Using ordering devices such as the frontal fireplace, rectilinear geometry, and the square grid, Wright created an informal arrangement of pavilions separated by corridors (circulation spines). The U-shaped plan embraces a series of formal and informal courtyards.

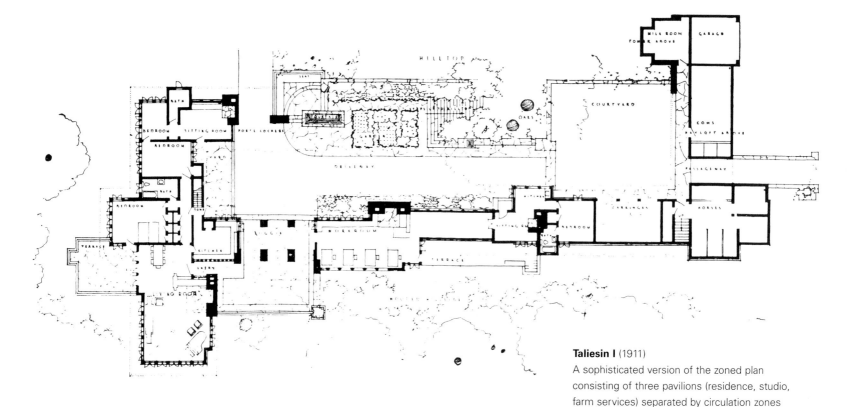

Taliesin I (1911)

A sophisticated version of the zoned plan consisting of three pavilions (residence, studio, farm services) separated by circulation zones (loggia and passageway). The rectilinear geometry and square grid give order as elements are deposed loosely in response to need and the hillside topography. The U-shaped plan turns inward, creating major and minor courtyards.

Frank Lloyd Wright Studio (1897)
The bi-nuclear plan with interior atrium in the main
vessel became the major plan type for public
buildings beginning in the 1890s. Analyzing the
functions of the studio hierarchically with the
drafting room as primary and the library as
secondary, Wright chose geometric figures of the
square and the octagon as separate units joined
by a transition space for entrance, circulation, and
study. Another contemporary example was the
Hillside Home School (1902).

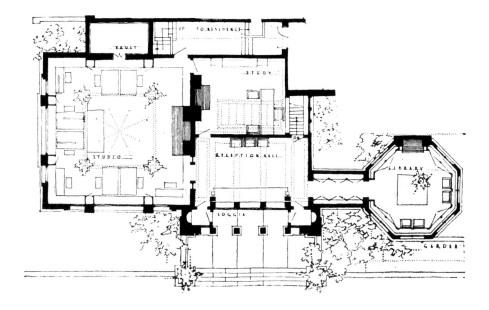

Unity Temple
(1906) One of the
most highly
resolved of the
bi-nuclear plans
with a primary
space (for church
services) and a
secondary space
(for Sunday school,
committee
meetings, and

social functions). Within the main two-story
hollow cube, Wright further rationalized the plan
with separate square stair towers at each corner.

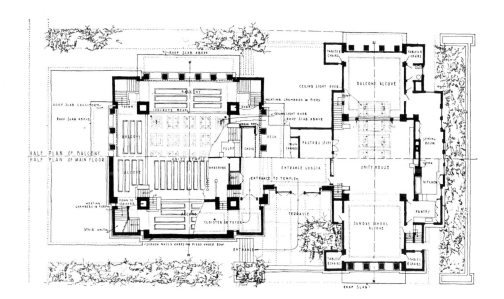

Prairie Houses

F. B. Henderson House

Elmhurst, Illinois 1901

With complete confidence, Prairie houses show off a clean set of forms and lines that stand out boldly from the picturesque massing of neighboring Tudor homes or the dignified symbolic ornament of Colonial homes.

Far right: Stairs lead from sidewalk up to the porch and front door. Right: The roof, porches, and windows simply and efficiently express themselves; Wright drew the beauty of the resulting house from the way he organized and balanced each.

Left: Sconces and leaded windows inside display a finer level of detail than do the finishes of the exterior to express their intimate relation to the lives of the residents. Above: The simple rounded bay of the library becomes a major element in the exterior composition. Below: The hallway connects the front door, living room, and stairs to the bedroom level above.
Next page: The living room with dining room at far right. Spaces flow together; the solid fireplace block holds the center, and the spaces—and the life of the residents—revolve around it.

Above: Bedroom with fireplace. Right: Built-in wardrobes. Next page: Wright gathered the windows of the Henderson house into continuous ribbons, contrasting with the flat, plastered walls. This relationship is maintained even at the left of this photograph where the dark window frames disappear but the band beneath the eaves continues as the house extends beyond its walls as an open-air terrace.

Frank W. Thomas House

Oak Park, Illinois 1901

Right: Many of Louis Sullivan's large commercial buildings used massive arches as a powerful element of their design, and Wright adapted the arch for use in several of his Prairie houses, including the Thomas House. Far right: The high ground level raises the living rooms to the second level. The ground floor includes servants' quarters.

Above: Like many (but not all) Prairie houses, the Thomas House emphasizes broad horizontal lines. It is in fact a three-story home. But by playing the broad foundation walls against the smaller, jutting wing of the dining room at right, a clean, low effect is achieved.

Above left: Beyond the large entry arch (seen on the previous pages) is this outdoor stair leading up to the front door, viewed from a broad terrace off the living room. Above right: The glassy entry hall on the second level.

Left: Living room looking toward hall. Above: Book alcove of living room.

Above left: Stairs. Above right: Dining room. Right: Wright's play with geometries is seen in the breakfast alcove off the dining room.
Its rectangular form is exaggerated by the square trim at its portal, contrasting with the hipped ceiling of the dining room proper. Next page:
The broad, clean forms of the Prairie house are startling, especially when compared with the Victorian-era brick house next door.

William G. Fricke House

Oak Park, Illinois 1901

By 1901, Wright had determined how he wanted a house to meet the ground, an important issue as Prairie houses self-consciously interact with their natural settings.

Far right: The simple motif of base, column, and cap formed the basic unit; Wright reinterpreted this motif for each element of the house, from the garden walls to the volume of the house as a whole. Unlike other horizontal three-story Prairie houses (such as the Robie House), the Fricke design still emphasizes its verticality; Wright experimented with these forms earlier.
Right: The low entry hall contrasts with the tall stair flooded by natural light.

Left: At this early stage in the evolution of the Prairie style, Wright uses broad-scaled, less ornate horizontal bands around the living room ceiling. Above left: The stairwell shows Wright's interlacing of flat plaster walls, horizontal and vertical wood ornament, three different levels and light to create a vivid space out of fundamental structural elements. Above right: The house itself is set on an articulated plinth of concrete foundation and stepped terraces. The structure was visually solid and balanced as a result.

Above: Wright's fireplaces form a catalog of his rich design imagination. In the Prairie years they were made of brick, but varied from extremely simple (as in the Fricke House) to commanding arches (as in the Heurtley house.) Right: Wright dramatically forces the observer to see these main spaces as a single unit by stretching a single ceiling over the lengthy dining room/breakfast room, while functionally separating them with a set of curtains on a lowered track.

Ward Willits House

Highland Park, Illinois 1901

Far right: Considered the first complete
Prairie house to be built, the Willits House
exhibits the basic elements of the type:
strong geometric volumes emphasized by
original wood trim, covered by a predominant
roof with wide eaves, a contrast of two-story
forms and one-story forms that help the
house claim its place on the landscape,
and a strong foundation line. These forms
constituted a firm break with tradition and
the creation of a new form reflecting both
the new suburban and industrial ages.
Right: Entry hall.

The wealth of ornamental invention in the interior shows how Wright used decoration to assertively define and link spaces. Left: The living room flows from the entry hall at right to the dining room at left. Above: The living room seen from dining room entry.

Left: Dining room. Above left: Angled built-in seating area at far end of dining room is complemented by the skylight overhead. Above right: Wright also designed the dining room chairs.

Above: With its corner filled with wrap-around glass windows, and with a balcony immediately off of it, this bedroom is designed to be open to nature. Right: Kitchen.

Left: A diamond-shaped lighting fixture is seen in the ceiling of the stair hall.

Above: The same stair hall includes a seating area halfway upstairs.

Above: A bedroom with an entire wall of windows. Below: By using new
construction methods, Wright left corners free of structure and filled with glass. Right: Bedroom.
Next page: Willits house with dining room wing and porch at left.

Susan Lawrence Dana House

Springfield, Illinois 1902

The large and lavishly budgeted Susan Lawrence Dana House, built for a progressive philanthropist living in the state capitol of Illinois, gave Wright the opportunity to develop the idea of "total design" in organic architecture. Exterior and interior spaces as well as furnishings were all under his eye and pencil.

Right: Entry reception hall. Far right: Front entry. Wright's elegant abstractions of form and materials are evident in the brick base and copper-clad roof of this façade, highlighted by bold coping atop the brick walls and pilasters. Next page: Exterior of gallery.

Above: The reception hall looking down into entry hall. Right: Entry hall. Next page: Dining room.

Left: Vaulted ceiling over dining room. Above: Seen as a whole, the Dana dining room was Wright's most completely executed design incorporating structure, space, ornament, furniture, and decorative pieces. The gallery overlooks the room.

Above left: Kitchen. Above right: Pantry and back stair. For most of Wright's Prairie houses,
the kitchen was the domain of servants and so was not integrated spatially into the family living spaces.
Right: Conservatory connecting reception hall with gallery.

Above: The sumac motif is seen in an art glass window. Below: The reception hall.
Right: Vault of gallery springs from a low beam.

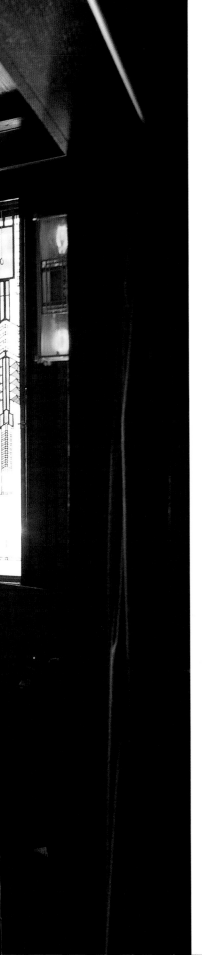

Left: Living room. Above: Bedroom with shallow pitched ceiling.

Above: Master bedroom with fireplace. Right: Master bedroom.

Left: Wright's striking composition balances the tall window frames of a staircase with an asymmetrical brick wall that anchors the house to the ground. The vaulted gallery is at right in the photograph. With such forms that shifted and changed, responding to the functions of the interior spaces, Wright created a complex yet unified whole. Above: This geometric pattern based on the sumac appears on fascias, windows, and other ornamental surfaces.

Arthur Heurtley House

Oak Park, Illinois 1902

Where the wings of the Willits House the year before sprawled over the land, the Heurtley House is reined into a single rectangular form beneath a magnificent widespread roof.

Right: The bravura arch around the living room fireplace is echoed in another that rises over the entry on the front façade, far right.

In the main public spaces of the house, Wright distinguished the living and dining rooms with distinct ceiling volumes. Left: Dining room. Above: View from living room toward dining room beyond. Below: Dining room looking toward living room.

Above: Bedroom. Right: Bathroom, remodeled.

Above: Kitchen. Below: Play room on ground floor. Right: Bedroom windows on rear façade
look out to the backyard. Balcony can be seen at left on second floor left. Bold forms similar to those
seen on the front façade, contained within the rectangular volume, are interpreted on the
back side of the house. Next page: Front elevation.

Darwin D. Martin House

Buffalo, New York 1903

With the design of Darwin Martin's house in Buffalo, New York, Wright took a further step in uniting structure and space. Here, the actual brick masonry construction is exposed, inside and out, with glass infill between structural columns and pylons.

Right: Window and wall. Far right: The main façade of the Martin house echoes the broad roof and balanced wings of the Willits house, but the differences are equally apparent. Instead of volumes skinned in plaster, these forms are sharply limned by the placement of brick pylons.

Left: Long foundation walls and tall pilasters create a spatial and structural composition.
Above: A window wall divides the living room and the large porch.

Above left: The entry hall at ground floor. Above right: The entry hall at second floor. Right: Through his studied placement of brick columns, the interior spaces are sharply defined as well as united. Extended outside onto terraces and a long pergola (destroyed many years ago) continuing from the entry hall, the structure also unites inside and outside. The result is an intricate three-dimensional space, stated and restated in a fabric of brick and wood surfaces and ornament.

Left: Bedroom windows. Above: Detail of a leaded glass window.

Darwin D. Martin
Gardener's Cottage (1905)

Though the construction of the house was troubled, Martin remained one of Wright's most loyal friends. As an executive at the Larkin Company, he persuaded the owner to hire Wright to design their Buffalo headquarters building, a landmark of Modern architecture. For his estate, Martin had Wright design several structures, including a cottage for his gardener.

Right: The cottage's foursquare simplicity echoed Wright's other forays into simplified construction meant to bring the benefits of Prairie design to the average middle-class family. Far right: The cottage entry and porch show the carefully balanced design of Wright's larger houses. Dining room windows are at right of the porch.

Left: Though a much more modest house than the Martin's main house, the gardener's cottage featured leaded glass windows.
Above left: The living room of the cottage. Above right: View from living room into dining room.

George Barton House

Buffalo, New York 1903

The basic elements of a typical Prairie house
are clearly visible in the Barton house, but
the variations illustrate how Wright adapted a
design for a specific client, site, materials,
budget—or for his own aesthetic exploration.

Far right: Instead of the articulated structural
pylons of the D.D. Martin house, Wright
gives the smaller Barton house on an
adjoining lot a solid brick first floor, punctured
by deep-set windows. Mrs. Barton was
Darwin Martin's sister. Right: Window detail.
Wright's fertile inventiveness is illustrated by
the variety of ornamental motifs he uses
throughout his houses for leaded glass
windows.

Left: View from entry hall to porch. Above: Entry hall looking toward dining room.

Left: Entry hall and stairs looking into living room. Above: A detail of wood trim on the living room ceiling. Below: Living room fireplace.

Above: Upstairs landing. Right: Bathroom for the four-bedroom house.

Mamah Borthwick and Edwin H. Cheney House

Oak Park, Illinois 1903

Through the skillful handling of the site and the house's proportions, Wright created a Prairie house that does indeed hug the flat ground of the Midwest. Though it appears to be a one-story house, a lower level, including garage, is sunken into the site.

Far right: The main living floor is slightly raised off the ground, a fact disguised by the terraces, plinths and foundation walls that spread out from the house into the ordinary suburban lot. Right: The delicate leaded glass patterns of the windows, inset with colored glass, modulate between the forest panorama outside and the interior.

The living room, dining room and library extend across the front of the house. United by the continuous hipped ceiling, they are functionally divided by columns and a flat lintel that divide the space. Windows ring three sides of the large living space, bringing in views of the suburban forest. Above left: Dining room. Above right: Fireplace. Below: Living room.

Above: The terrace leads directly off living room. Right: Bedroom.

William A. Glasner House

Glencoe, Illinois 1905

The ground-hugging forms of the Glasner house prefigure the straightforward lines of houses later in the twentieth century. But beneath the forthright roofline, the walls of the house form a collection of octagonal at right and rectangular rooms. Set on the edge of a sloping ravine, the house looks out into a forest.

Right: The front door is set into an angled intersection between the octagonal library at left and the living room. Far right: Front door is seen at the center of the photograph. Master bedroom wing is at right.

Left: The living room ceiling's varied pattern of thick and thin wood trim differs from the trim of the Coonley and other Wright houses. Above left: The fireplace divides the living room on the right from the kitchen on the left. The distinct horizontal lines of the board and batten lower walls and the roof eave emphasize the house's closeness to the ground.
Above right: Wright repeated the octagonal bay at both ends of the house. This bay is a sewing room off the master bedroom. Below: Living room looking toward octagonal library.

A. W. Gridley House

Batavia, Illinois 1906

A variation on the cruciform plan Wright often favored, the Gridley house relies on the simplicity of contrasting plaster and wood trim.

Far right: The gridded pattern of the windows placed strategically against the light plaster walls add ornamental interest; note their placement at corners to de-emphasize the traditional structural purpose of the corners. The proportions divide the house between a large ground floor and a thin ribbon representing the second floor. Right: Entry hall and front door.

Left: The living room fireplace uses the contrasting bands of colored brick seen in the Heurtley house's exterior.
Above: Stair landing at the second floor.

Above left: Dining room windows wrap around three sides of the room to create walls of glass. Above right: Kitchen.
Right: The dining room has a built-in sideboard that follows the spare decoration of the rest of the house. Next page: The two-story wing
at right is balanced by a one-story wing at left. The front door is hidden at the intersection of the two two-story wings.

Ferdinand and Emily Tomek House

Riverside, Illinois 1907

Wright's boldly Modern reinterpretation of
traditional residential forms is obvious in the
Tomek House. The roof is the primary
defining form, cantilevered far beyond the
last support to create a free-hanging canopy
over an open-air terrace, not the traditional
wrap-around verandah.

Far right: The house's asymmetric
composition may echo the picturesquely
unbalanced wings of many suburban Tudor
designs, but here the bold abstraction of
the walls, tower, and roofs are their own
aesthetic. With the main living rooms
raised to the second level, the first floor
becomes a blank wall, further violating
the standards of conventional design.
Right: Entry stair leading from ground to
second-story living room.

Above left: A long gallery lined with windows links the living room to the dining room. Above right: Living room.
Doors flanking alcove at end of room lead to the large covered terrace. Right: Breakfast alcove at end of dining room.

Left: Master bedroom on third floor. Above: Window detail. Next page: The dining room end of the house.
The front door is at right. The broad cantilevered eave thrusts far beyond the end of the house.

Avery and Queene Coonley House

Riverside, Illinois 1907

Though now considered one of Wright's
early masterpieces, some critics considered
the Coonley house "freakish" when it was
built. Such comments give us a glimpse of
how startlingly new and different the
design appeared.

Far right: The main entry is almost invisible
in the shadows of the bridge between two
of the house's wings. The main living spaces
are on the second floor. Right: These steps
just inside the front door lead up to the
main floor.

Left: Living room. The broad fireplace centers the room. Murals on the walls on either side artfully mirror the panoramic view of the river and forest seen from the living room's phalanx of windows, seen above.

Left: The asymmetrical balance of the dining room between the brick fireplace and the glass window walls is echoed in the varied wood trim on the ceiling. Above left: Beyond the dining room's fireplace, the stair landing at the top of the main entry stairs can be seen. Above right: At the top of the stairs, a skylight with art glass floods the landing with light. Beyond, the space flows into the spacious living room.

Above: Kitchen. Right: Guest bedroom. Next page: The living room wing thrusts out from the main building.
The dining room is at left, the bedrooms at right.

Coonley Bedroom Wing (1907)

Far left: The leaded glass windows reiterate the large and small scale of the house's rectilinear geometries. Left above: The master bedroom wing. Left below: Sitting room.

Above: Window patterns are seen again in the decorative surface of the exterior's second floor.
Right: The hallway in bedroom wing.

Above: The dressing room in master suite. Right: As a large estate for a wealthy family,
the Coonley house has many suites with dressing rooms and bedrooms.

Coonley Coach House (1911)

The Coonley estate includes smaller cottages for employees, a coach house, and a playhouse for their children.

Far left: The coach house has been converted into a distinct residence. Above left: Coach house living room. Below left: Kitchen. Next page: The auxiliary buildings repeat the proportions and materials of the main house to create a fully integrated compound.

Coonley Gardener's Cottage (1911)

Two views of the small Gardener's Cottage, built in 1911, on the Coonley estate. The one-story, two-bedroom cottage was later echoed in Wright's efforts to create affordable, prefabricated housing. Below left: Living room.

Coonley Playhouse (1912)

In 1912, Mrs. Queene Ferry Coonley asked Wright to design a playhouse for her children, where she also operated a small school.

Far left: Wright's delightful designs for the windows, including abstract balloons, match the purpose of the playhouse and are among his most famous art glass designs. Above left: Long clerestory windows fill the room with light. Below left: One end of the playhouse is raised for use as a stage, with a proscenium. The building is now a residence. Next page: The exterior of the playhouse. When compared with the original house, the flat room and distinctive trellises extending from the structure mark a shift for Wright.

Frederick C. Robie House

Chicago, Illinois 1908

The Robie House is one of Frank Lloyd
Wright's most daring designs. Though built
on a narrow urban site, the house is private
and open.

Far right: The astonishing span of the
cantilevered roof over the living room terrace
proclaims the theme of a house stretching
out to the horizon, and establishes the image
of shelter. Right: A window detail
incorporates diagonal lines as a counterpoint
to the rectilinear lines of the house.

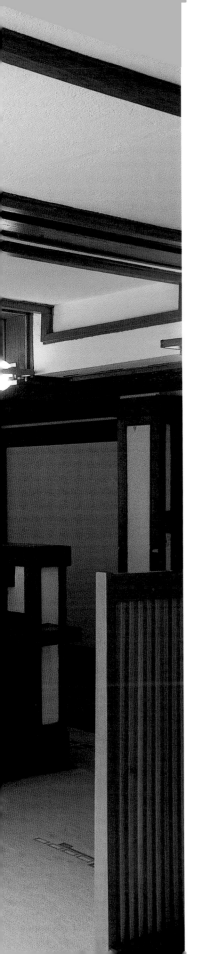

Left: Stairs from the front door below divide the dining room from the living room beyond the chimney.
Above: Hemispherical lighting fixtures contrast with the angles of the rest of the design.

Above: The living room fireplace. Right: The living room is lined with windows on three sides.
A built-in seating area is seen at the far end of the room.

Left: The three-story house includes a ground floor playroom and outdoor terrace, and the living and dining room on the second floor. Above: The smaller third floor has three bedrooms. Long terraces make the outdoors accessible from most rooms.

G. C. Stockman House

Mason City, Iowa 1908

Unlike the lavish Darwin Martin, Dana, or Coonley houses, the Stockman House is a modest but solid middle class house. The aesthetics and practical advantages of the Prairie style are evident nonetheless. Wright was eager to spread the gospel of his new architecture to all levels of society. Based on a concept for a fireproof all-concrete structure, the windowless corner pilasters reflect the slablike simplicity of Wright's 1904 Unity Temple, which was actually constructed of concrete.

Far right: The porte cochere entry with its wide cantilever adds a complementary form to balance the severe symmetry of the main block. Right: Dining room.

The most prominent aspects of Prairie house architecture—for example, the connection between indoors and out—are evident in the banks of French doors that open to the porch from the living room. Left: The living room fireplace with French doors to the verandah beyond. Above: Living room. The entry is a few steps down at center left of photograph.

Above: One of the four bedrooms upstairs. Right: Dining room. Interiors show a simplification though the ornamental motifs of leaded glass and wood trim seen in the larger estates are still present.

Edward Boynton House

Rochester, New York 1908

The long rectangular block of the Boynton
House stretches deep into its suburban lot.

Right: The broad winglike roofs jut out
toward the street, softened by planters built
integrally to the architecture. Wright placed
the front door halfway down the side of the
house. Far right: A view toward street. The
windows of the protruding bay flood the stair
hall with light. The carefully plotted angles,
horizontal overhangs and vertical walls of the
design are thus seen as the visitor moves
around and past them and their ever-changing
relationship to each other.

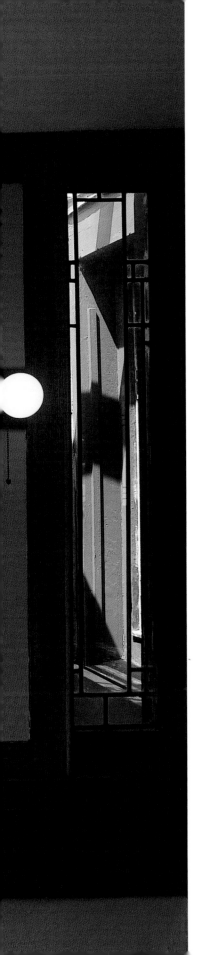

Left: Dining room window detail with integral planter. Above: The verandah off the
living room has been enclosed. Below: The interior of the verandah.

The dining room is a dynamic space. Left: A low nook thrusts out along the side, leaving a high clerestory window to flood the center of the room with light. To balance the leaded glass windows, a series of artificial lighting fixtures are set into the ceiling. Above left: Wright was personally involved in the design and construction of this house, visiting it during construction. Above right: He designed the furniture and other ornamental elements, including the illuminated post-tops for the dining room table. Next page: Confident asymmetrical design of the living room shows Wright's mastery of proportion and space.

Above: Pantry. Right: The pantry with a view into the dining room at left of photograph.

Left: Bedroom. Above: Top of the stair landing.

Above: The bathroom off the bedroom. Right: Bedroom.

Isabel Roberts House

River Forest, Illinois 1908

Right: The sculptural character of Wright's architecture is seen in this composition of horizontal and vertical planes, of solids and voids. Far right: The front door is on the side of the house; Wright often de-emphasized the entry. Originally surfaced in plaster with wood trim like the Willits House, the brick facing was added in the 1920s.

Left: Living room. Wright replaced the original pine trim with mahogany in a 1955 remodeling.
Above: The upper balcony overlooks the living room.

Above: Dining room. Right: Detail of a dining room lighting fixture.

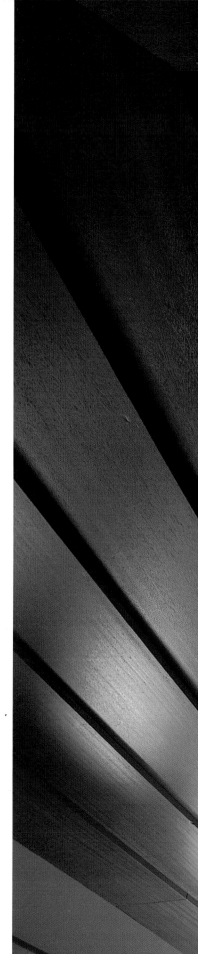

Left: A balcony was added in 1955 to the master bedroom. Above: Master bedroom.

Emily and George Stewart House

Montecito, California 1909

California played a large role in Wright's later career, but the Stewart House was the first he structure he built in the Golden State. It was designed for a Fresno family desiring a house near the ocean.

Right: Like the George Millard House (1906) in Highland Park, Illinois, the finish material of the Stewart House is wood, represented in broad horizontal board and batten lines. Far right: Though many Prairie houses use extensive glass, the spaciousness, openness, and light particularly suited the benign climate of coastal California.

Left: The interlocking geometric volumes that characterize many Prairie houses allow the Stewart's living room to enjoy light from a high, inset clerestory. Above: A balcony overlooks the two-story living room. The present furnishings are a reminder that the Prairie and Craftsman styles took root at the same time and shared a philosophical interest in a straightforward expression of natural materials.

Above and right: The study. Though Wright still used windows as an opportunity for a delicate ornamental filigree to complement the house's lines, here they are less ornate than in earlier Prairie houses. The screen at right allows for air to flow through the house.

Left: The horizontal trellis extending from the top of the living room's bay window is a late invention of the Prairie style, but would continue to be a Wrightian motif for the rest of his career. Above left: Second story windows look out on balconies. Above right: The wood steps repeat the rhythms and details of the board and batten siding.

Edward and Florence Irving House

DeCatur, Illinois 1909

The distinctive proportions of the large Irving
house reflect the intricate play of volumes
that defines the Prairie house.

Right: A planter at the front of house.
Far right: The lamp post's steel, glass, brick
and coping each retain their own character
while fitting together into a bold design. In
the same way, the red tile roof, the bands of
windows, the vertical brick pylons, and the
second floor's horizontal white plaster
projections each retain their character, while
working together in an interlocking abstract
composition.

Above: The space of the main floor is shaped by the placement of the brick chimney and large columns.
Right: The ornamental grillwork of the columns veil structure, radiators, and storage cabinets.

Above: Dining room. Left: The same design used in the ornamental glass for the exterior
windows is repeated in the cabinet doors of the dining room sideboard.

Above left: Door to porch. Above right: Confident vertical and horizontal planes of varied thickness, complemented by thin strips of trim, create the Prairie style's three-dimensional architecture.

Above left: Stairs. Above right: The upstairs hallway with skylight.

Next page: Front elevation.

Harry S. Adams House

Oak Park, Illinois 1913

Wright's last Prairie house built in Oak Park shows the simplification of his ornament and forms as he closed out the Prairie years and moved on to the next phase of his career.

Right: The brick house contrasts the two-story block with the low porte cochere that balances the design. Far right: A long eave shelters visitors walking up to the front door.

Above: The living room with windows flanking the fireplace. Below: An art glass door.
Right: The living room with built-in couch looks toward enclosed verandah beyond.

Left: Dining room. Instead of gathering windows together to create a window wall,
Wright uses tall, individual openings in the far wall. Above: A built-in sideboard shows Wright's
continuing interest in geometries to give form.

Ravine Bluffs Development

Glencoe, Illinois 1915

The challenge of designing individual houses naturally lead Wright to the challenge of designing an entire neighborhood. The Prairie house required a studied placement of each of the houses in the development to bring out their interrelated qualities. Thanks to his lawyer, Sherman Booth, Wright finally had an opportunity to build several houses at once at Ravine Bluffs.

Right: The neighborhood included Wright-designed entry markers and a bridge. Far right: The house he designed for Booth was the largest of the group.

Wright's trend toward simplification is seen in the Booth House. Left: The white plaster surfaces are modeled into horizontal eaves and protruding balconies. Above left: The study.
Above right: The enclosed porch. Below right: The enclosed porch looking toward living room. Wright's travels to Japan influenced the design of his sliding glass partitions, which are thin and light.
Below left: The composition of the exterior relies less on expressing the structure (as in the Darwin Martin House) than on an arrangement of abstract forms similar to the Gale House (1909).
Next page: The Kier House. Booth had Wright design five other houses in 1915 in the neighborhood for rental properties along the curving suburban lane.

Above: The strong interlocking volumes of the Root House convey the sense of solidity and connection to the earth. Below: The Ross House. Right: The Kissam House.

Left: The Perry House. Above: Wright-designed entry markers.

Taliesin I

Spring Green, Wisconsin 1911 (remodeled in 1914 and 1925)

At Taliesin, a dramatic site and the challenge of designing a home for himself and his lover, Mamah Cheney, in his beloved Wisconsin hometown of Spring Green inspired Wright in a way no other house had. Though the vocabulary of masonry pillars and broad shingled roofs is the same as the Prairie houses, he used the sloping site, native stone, and a complex mix of purposes (home, studio, working farm) to create a masterpiece.

Right: The sloping brow-of-the-hill site creates views of the house and landscape. Far right: Taliesin was rebuilt twice after damaging fires in 1914 and 1925. Like his Oak Park home, Wright also used this home as a laboratory and experimented with the house throughout the rest of his lifetime.

Left: The main living room and the Wrights' bedroom suite overlooks the rolling hills.
Above: This view balcony off the Wright's suite was extended through the years. Below: A view from the top of the hill toward the main porte cochere entry.

Above left: The horizontal lines of the ashlar masonry are picked up in the lines of the French doors. Above right: Clerestory windows bring light into the living room from above to balance the light from the surrounding windows. Below: Oriental artifacts, musical instruments, natural flowers blended with the textures of stone and wood. Right: Living room.

Left: Sitting room. Above: The house was built as Wright's personal home, but after 1932 it was also the home of Wright's community, the Taliesin Fellowship, which drew together young architects, craftspeople, artists, and musicians to learn from the master architect and to work as his architectural office. Below: The rambling house includes many large and small, sunny and intimate spaces.

Above: Parts of the large home were remodeled many times over the years, reflecting the latest ideas Wright was interested in. Below: One of the home's later bedrooms. Right: Instead of creating an entire wall of glass to unite the outdoor balcony with the bedroom, Wright incorporated a wood screen to modulate between indoors and outdoors.

Left: Wright used varying heights in his spaces to create drama, to direct attention to a view, and to bring in light.

Above left: This bedroom (added after the 1925 fire) uses natural stone and different colors of plaster. Above right: The rough stone around the fireplace gives way to smooth plaster above.

Above: The dominant symmetries of many of Wright's Prairie houses gives way to complex asymmetrical arrangements of structure and space at Taliesin. Right: Dining room, kitchen, farm buildings, and housing for his apprentices cap the hill. While the broad eaves of the Prairie houses are evident here, the composition is more abstract.

Left: The intricacies of the wood trim patterns of the ceiling of the Coonley and other earlier designs give way to a bolder simplicity that is still rich in pattern. Above: Dining area. Next page: Wright retreated from Chicago and Oak Park's social life in 1911 to live in relative isolation in Spring Green. The move suited him, but made it more difficult to keep his architectural practice active. Twenty-five years later he would make yet another move even farther from the centers of the architectural profession when he built another Taliesin in Scottsdale, Arizona.

Exiles, Lovers, and Tourists: Florence, 1910

By Kathryn Smith

Nature!
We are encompassed and enveloped by her,
powerless to penetrate deeper.
Unbidden and unwarmed she takes us up in
the round of her Dance and sweeps
along with us, until exhausted we fall
from her Arms.

— From "A Hymn to Nature," by Johann Wolfgang von Goethe,
translated by Mamah Borthwick and Frank Lloyd Wright

By the fall of 1909, the smoldering love affair between Frank Lloyd Wright and Mamah Borthwick Cheney had reached a turning point. An attraction had begun as early as 1903 when Wright was drawn to Mamah during the design and construction of a new house in Oak Park for herself and her husband, Edwin, an electrical engineer.[1] By 1908, the couple openly declared their love to their families and sought release from their marriages. "She told her husband one year before she went away with me," Wright recalled, "that she would go with me married or not whenever I could take her. Marriage was never a condition with her anymore than it was with me—except that in order to work I felt this must take place when it might if it might. It seemed at one time (owing to requests of her husband solely) as though this were to be made a condition—and I so misunderstood it myself for a time, but this was never her stipulation nor did she ever hide behind it."[2] Wright's wife, Catherine, refused to accept her husband's infidelity, holding firm to the idea that the situation would ultimately resolve itself in her favor. "I would in any case have separated from

Catherine," he declared, "though I might have continued under the same roof with her for the sake of the children—but even that … I was determined not to do."[3]

After being asked to contribute to a small picture book series on twentieth-century architecture by German publisher, Wasmuth Verlag, Wright countered by proposing a luxurious portfolio of his work to be designed, financed, and owned by himself. Banking that profits from the publication would generate much needed income to offset his rising expenses, he decided to seize the opportunity to go to Berlin with Mamah to oversee production. On September 20, he bade his family good-bye, turned his practice over to a minor architect, set sail with Mamah from New York, and was registered in a Berlin hotel by early November. An enterprising (and perhaps tipped off) *Chicago Tribune* reporter discovered their presence and the scandal of their break with conventional middle-class morality was emblazoned across the newspapers. "You understand, of course, that everything would be condoned by the public *if only* we were married, that is the point," Mamah revealed to a confidante sometime later, "But Frank, of course, cannot marry as he has not been divorced. Neither of us has ever felt, of course, that that had the slightest possible significance in the 'morality' or 'immorality' of our actions, but it has *all* the significance in the newspaper-public consciousness."[4]

Preoccupied with the thought that they would be hounded and harassed by the press, they split up and eventually sought to settle

where they would appear inconspicuous. By February 1910, Wright had arrived in Florence, Italy, and begun a search for a place to share with Mamah. After a few months with his son, Lloyd Wright, and a draftsman, Taylor Woolley, redrawing plans and perspectives of his selected works, Mamah joined him at the Villino Belvedere, a small cream-colored house built into a hillside in Fiesole overlooking Florence. With the exception of excursions of a few days or weeks, they would remain there through the summer until Wright made preparations to return to Chicago.

They were a compatible couple. When they fled Chicago, the Wisconsin-born architectural theorist and Japanese art collector Wright was forty-two; the college-educated Mamah, a student of German literature, was two years younger. Outgrowing both his rural upbringing and the provincialism of Oak Park, Wright had gained national prominence as the leading innovator of a new school of Midwest architecture (later referred to as Prairie School architecture or Prairie style), or as he would have preferred to call it, Organic Architecture. The portfolio he created in Fiesole—a survey of his first fifteen years of practice—would become the most important architectural publication of the twentieth century. Having been associated in sin—though always in separate homes—the clandestine couple was at last free to explore the passion of their first year alone together; but they were more than lovers, their intense union was forged by mutual interests in art and literature.

By this time, Wright had participated in two exhibitions of Japanese prints and published several essays, and he collaborated on—or gently edited phrases of—Mamah's translations.[5] Without domestic entanglements, they were both free that summer to concentrate on their own writing. Wright was composing a theoretical tract as an introduction to his portfolio, *Ausgeführte Bauten und Entwürfe von Frank Lloyd Wright* (Berlin, 1911). Mamah had recently encountered the treatises of the Swedish feminist, Ellen Key, while traveling in France. After securing the author's cooperation, she immersed herself in Swedish beginning translations of *The Morality of Woman and other Essays* (Chicago, 1911) and *Love and Ethics* (Chicago, 1912).[6] Financed by Wright and printed under his supervision, these three publications became an outgrowth of their literary partnership.

Villino Belvedere on Via Guiseppe Verdi, Fiesole, 1910. Special Collections, University of Utah Library.

VILLINO BELVEDERE

Italian architects, Giampaolo and Filippo Fici, noted that the Villino Belvedere, adjacent to the much grander Villa Belvedere, appeared for the first time on an 1869 document and by stylistic evidence dated its construction to the middle of the 1800s.[7] By the twentieth century, an Englishwoman, Elisa Illingworth, owned the residence as an income property, now located off the Via Giuseppe Verdi.

Wright may have known about the villino before renting it for the spring and summer, six months between March and August 1910. On first arriving in Florence, while he resided at the Villino Fortuna on the south bank of the Arno River, just below the Piazzale Michelangelo, he probably made the acquaintance of members of the Anglo-American community, who provided referrals. Evidence that he had met Illingworth by February is revealed in a drawing he made for a proposed Italian villa for his own use. The marginal note reads: "Villa Florence Italy,

Via Verdi—Madame Illingworth—Feb 1910." No information survives to explain why Wright designed his own villa in Florence; though the modest villino was hardly more than a rustic house—not comparable to the more splendid villas nearby.

But there is no doubt that his romantic idyll increased his appreciation of what he called the "little eyrie on the brow of the mountain above Fiesole."[8] Afterwards, he retained a vivid memory of the "small solid door framed in the solid white blank wall with the massive green door opening toward the narrow Via Verdi itself."[9] The house terraced steeply down the hillside and off the main rooms opened onto a high walled garden. There "by the pool arbored under climbing masses of yellow roses" was set " a white cloth on the small stone table near the little fountain."[10] And the table set for two looked down on "the pink and white Florence spreading in the valley of the Arno

below—the whole fertile bosom of the earth seemingly lying in the drifting mists or shining clear and marvelous in this Italian sunshine—opalescent—iridescent."[11]

EXILES, TOURISTS, AND LOVERS

In Florence and its surrounding towns, there was a long history of foreign exiles, tourists, and lovers finding refuge. "How many souls seeking release from real or fancied woes," Wright contemplated later, "have sheltered on the slopes of Fiesole!"[12] Although there is no evidence that Wright and Mamah took part in "... the often high-minded hedonistic but intellectually stimulating life of the Anglo-American community in Florence ... [a] society of high ideals, of sexual intrigue, of flouted conventions, and of patrician aspirations," it was a locale where they certainly had much more in common with their neighbors than they did in Oak Park.[13]

The Stein Family at Villa Bardi on Via Giuseppe Verdi, Fiesole, 1908. Sarah Stein is seated in the foreground with her husband, Michael, and their son, Allan, behind her; Gertrude Stein is to the left, with Leo Stein seated at back between two unknown friends.
Yale Collection of American Literature, Beinecke Rare Book and Manuscript Library. Yale University, New Haven.

In nearby Settignano, the imperious art connoisseur, Bernhard Berenson, lived at the Villa I Tatti; a Harvard-educated scholar of Italian Renaissance painting, he had married his mistress of ten years, Mary Costelloe, after her husband's fortuitous death. Berenson and his wife both had a compelling interest in Italian art; he spent his time writing such seminal volumes as *The Florentine Painters of the Renaissance* (1896) and *The Study and Criticism of Italian Art* (1901) while Mary contributed articles on art criticism to journals and magazines. Berenson conducted a salon that indulged foreign lovers of the arts, especially moneyed eccentrics of various sexual preferences.

Perhaps the most flamboyant of these was the exotic, and virtually legendary, Mabel Dodge, who sought to recreate the life of Renaissance Italy rather than study it. With the help of her architect husband, the wealthy American transformed the Villa Curonia in Arcetri—an extravagant stage set complete with a ninety-foot long grand salon and an Italian garden overflowing with cypresses, jasmine, gardenias, and white peacocks—into "a crown on the gray-green land."[14] Dressed in stiff crimson and gold brocaded coats and a white chiffon turban, she held elaborate candle-lit fêtes and intimate dinners with such luminaries as the poet Gabriele D'Annunzio; the French novelist Andre Gide; Pen Browning, the son of Robert and Elizabeth; and Leo and Gertrude Stein. "The dead Florentines," she remarked, "are thick in the dust all about on nights like these."[15]

While Mabel Dodge and others such as the notorious bi-sexual courtesan, Princess Anne-Marie Ghika (formerly Liane de Pougy) and her companion, Florence Blood, residing at the sumptuous Medicean Villa Gamberaia, lived an ingrown life of cultivated leisure, many exiles and tourists were hard-working writers like Gertrude and Leo Stein. As a serious student of Renaissance art and an avid collector of Japanese prints, Leo's uncanny level of connoisseurship had led him to the next step of aesthetic development: the discovery of the modern painters Paul Cezanne, Henri Matisse, and Pablo Picasso. Leo, who first moved to Florence in 1900 to write a book on Mantegna, returned again and again, finally choosing Fiesole for his spring and summer holidays. Always in the company of his sister, Gertrude, and often with his brother, Michael and his family, Leo rented the comfortable Villa Bardi on the Via Giuseppe Verdi. In May, 1910 Gertrude and her new love, Alice B. Toklas, joined her brother, only a short distance from the Villino Belvedere. Settled comfortably in Fiesole to write, like Wright and Mamah, Gertrude spent the summer at work on her monumental novel, *The Making of Americans* (Paris, 1925), with occasional trips to other Italian cities. Although living on the same street, there is no record that Wright and Mamah ever met Gertrude and Alice; but it is fascinating to speculate that they might have passed each other more than once in the piazza.

TALIESIN

Wright's voluntary exile in rural Fiesole corresponded with the financial collapse of his maternal relatives, the Lloyd Jones family in southern Wisconsin. A clan of Welsh Unitarians, his aunts and uncles had settled a pastoral valley in the 1860s and prospered with adjoining farms. In the midst of the fields and meadows, his two maiden aunts, Ellen and Jane, had founded the Hillside Home School drawing children from nearby cities. But by 1909, it was all in jeopardy; bankruptcy was looming over the school and the farmland was at risk of passing out of family hands due to the deaths of two of Wright's uncles, James and John. While contemplating his next move, his mother

wrote to him of the crisis in southern Wisconsin. In the same letter that he informs her he would be leaving Europe in September, he expresses a desire to return to the valley to farm. "But my situation is too discouraging to contemplate such a luxury," he added. Nevertheless, within a year, he is at work designing and constructing a new house and studio, Taliesin, for himself and Mamah adjacent to the ancestral lands. By late 1911, Mamah, now divorced from her husband, "made a choice in harmony with my own soul and what I believed to be Frank Wright's happiness," as she told a friend. As Wright returned to his practice, Mamah turned again to translation, explaining, "The house is now, however, practically finished and my time again free. Mr. Wright has his studio incorporated into the house and we both will be busy with our own work, with absolutely no outside interests on my part."[16]

Although the six-month idyll in Fiesole was more an escape than a solution, it was an extremely key episode in Wright's creation of a new self. Taliesin, like the Villino Belvedere, was built into a hillside overlooking a bucolic valley with a view recalling the "fertile bosom of the earth seemingly lying in the drifting mists or shining clear and marvelous in this … sunshine" of the previous summer. Here Mamah found that the "attempt to do what we believed right had succeeded. I can now say that we have … the entire respect of the community in which we live."[17] But this ideal attained was to be dramatically cut short in the tragic fire and murders of August 1914 when Mamah, her two children, and four others lost their lives at the hand of an insane servant. With Mamah's death, the significance of the Florentine experience was lost; but, preserving her memory, Wright turned to Taliesin to rebuild. •

NOTES

[1] Mamah Bouton Borthwick (1869–1914), the youngest of four children, was born in Iowa to Almira and Marcus Smith Borthwick, an architect for the Chicago and Northwestern Railroad. Following her childhood in Oak Park, she obtained a B.A. (1892) and an M.A. (1893) from the University of Michigan, majoring in languages. After her marriage to Edwin Cheney (1899), the couple commissioned Wright to design their new house in Oak Park. Her two children, John (born in 1903) and Martha (born in 1906), grew up in a household that included Mamah's sister, Lizzie Borthwick, a public school teacher; her mother-in-law, Almira; and live-in servants including a governess. In 1905, Mamah enrolled in the University of Chicago.

[2] Frank Lloyd Wright to Anna Lloyd Wright, July 4, 1910, Villino Belvedere, Fiesole. Frank Lloyd Wright Archives, Scottsdale, Arizona.

[3] Ibid.

[4] Mamah Bouton Borthwick to Ellen Key, n.d. (early 1912). Ellen Key Archive, Manuscripts Department, Royal Library, National Library of Sweden, Stockholm. For further background on Borthwick's translations of Key, see Alice T. Friedman, "Frank Lloyd Wright and Feminism, Mamah Borthwick's Letters to Ellen Key," *Journal of the Society of Architectural Historians*, 61, no. 2 (Jun 2002), 140-151 and Lena Johannesson, "Ellen Key, Mamah Bouton Borthwick and Frank Lloyd Wright: Notes on the Historiography of Non-existing History," *Nora: Nordic Journal of Women's Studies* 3, no. 2 (1995), 126-136.

[5] *Hiroshige: An Exhibition of Colour Prints from the Collection of Frank Lloyd Wright* (Art Institute of Chicago, 1906); "In the Cause of Architecture," *Architectural Record* 23 (March 1908), 115-221. In addition to the Hiroshige exhibition, Wright contributed to Loan Exhibition of Colour Prints, also at the Art Institute, 1908. Wright designed the installation and also was the major lender.

[6] Wright is credited as co-translator for *Love and Ethics*.

[7] Giampaolo Fici and Filippo Fici, *Frank Lloyd Wright: Fiesole, 1910* (Florence: Minello Sani, 1992), 14.

[8] Alan Crawford, "Ten Letters from Frank Lloyd Wright to Charles Robert Ashbee," *Architectural History: Journal of the Society of Architectural Historians of Great Britain* 13 (1970): 67.

[9] Frank Lloyd Wright, *An Autobiography* (New York: Duell, Sloan and Pearce, 1943), 165.

[10] Ibid.

[11] Crawford, "Ten Letters," 67.

[12] *Autobiography*, 164.

[13] Richard M. Dunn, *Geoffrey Scott and the Berenson Circle: Literary and Aesthetic Life in the Early 20th Century* (Lewiston, Queenston, Lampeter: The Edwin Mellen Press, 1998), xix.

[14] Mabel Dodge Luhan, *European Experiences* (New York: Harcourt, Brace, 1935), 137.

[15] Ibid., 158.

[16] Borthwick to Key, n.d., (ca. December 1911). National Library of Sweden.

[17] Borthwick to Key, November 10, 1912. National Library of Sweden.

HOUSE LIST

Edited by Alan Hess

This list includes the original client's name, and the earliest known date when a project was first conceived, commissioned, or designed, as confirmed by The Frank Lloyd Wright Foundation. This order is intended to roughly approximate the evolution of Wright's design ideas as they unfolded on his drafting table.

1900

Edward R. Hills Remodeling
Oak Park, Illinois

B. Harley Bradley House
Kankakee, Illinois

Warren Hickox House
Kankakee, Illinois

Henry Wallis Cottage
Delavan, Wisconsin

1901

F. B. Henderson House
Elmhurst, Illinois

William G. Fricke and Emma Martin House
Oak Park, Illinois

Frank W. Thomas House
(The Harem)
Oak Park, Illinois
Marion Mahony

E. Arthur Davenport House
River Forest, Illinois

1902

Ward Willits House
Highland Park, Illinois

William E. Martin House
Oak Park, Illinois

Susan Lawrence Dana House
Springfield, Illinois

Arthur Heurtley House
Oak Park, Illinois

George Gerts Cottage
Whitehall, Michigan

Walter Gerts Cottage
Whitehall, Michigan

George W. Spencer House
Delavan, Wisconsin

Charles S. Ross House
Delavan, Wisconsin

A. W. Hebert House
Evanston, Illinois / altered

1903

Francis W. and Mary Little House I
Peoria, Illinois

J. J. Walser Jr. House
Chicago, Illinois

Kenwood Remodeling
Chicago, Illinois

Darwin D. Martin House
Buffalo, New York

George Barton House
Buffalo, New York

Mamah Borthwick and Edwin H. Cheney House
Oak Park, Illinois

William Heath House
Buffalo, New York

1905

Harvey P. Sutton House
McCook, Nebraska

Mary M. W. Adams House
Highland Park, Illinois

William A. Glasner House
Glencoe, Illinois

Charles A. Brown House
Evanston, Illinois

Thomas P. Hardy House
Racine, Wisconsin

Darwin D. Martin Gardener's Cottage
Buffalo, New York

A. P. Johnson House
Delavan, Wisconsin

Laura R. Gale Cottages
Whitehall, Michigan

1906

Burton J. Westcott House
Springfield, Ohio

Peter A. Beachy House
Oak Park, Illinois
Barry Byrne

Frederick D. Nichols House
Flossmoor, Illinois

P. D. Hoyt House
Geneva, Illinois

A. W. Gridley House
Batavia, Illinois

Grace Fuller House
Glencoe, Illinois / demolished

K. C. DeRhodes House
South Bend, Indiana

George M. Millard House
Highland Park, Illinois

1907

Ferdinand and Emily Tomek House
Riverside, Illinois

George Fabyan Remodeling
Geneva, Illinois

Andrew Porter House (Tanyderi)
Spring Green, Wisconsin

Avery and Queene Coonley House
Riverside, Illinois

Stephen Hunt House
LaGrange, Illinois

1908

Frederick C. Robie House
Chicago, Illinois

G. C. Stockman House
Mason City, Iowa

Raymond W. Evans House
Chicago, Illinois

L. K. Horner House
Chicago, Illinois / demolished

Eugene Gilmore House
Madison, Wisconsin

Edward Boynton House
Rochester, New York

Meyer May House
Grand Rapids, Michigan

Walter V. Davidson House
Buffalo, New York

Isabel Roberts House
River Forest, Illinois

1909

Laura R. Gale House
Oak Park, Illinois

Hiram Baldwin House
Kenilworth, Illinois

Como Orchard Summer Colony Cottages
Darby, Montana

Frank H. Baker House
Wilmette, Illinois

Oscar Steffens House
Chicago, Illinois / demolished

William H. Copeland Remodeling
Oak Park, Illinois

Emily and George Stewart House
Montecito, California

J. Kibben Ingalls House
River Forest, Illinois

Edward and Florence Irving House
Decatur, Illinois
Marion Mahony and Herman von Holst

Ingwald Moe House
Gary, Indiana
American Systems Homes

1910

Jessie R. Ziegler House
Frankfort, Kentucky

1911

O. B. Balch House
Oak Park, Illinois

Herbert Angster House
Lake Bluff, Illinois / demolished

Taliesin I
Spring Green Wisconsin
1914 remodeling
1925 remodeling

Walter Gerts Remodeling
River Forest, Illinois

Sherman M. Booth Cottage
Glencoe, Illinois
Ravine Bluffs Development

1912

Coonley Playhouse
Riverside, Illinois

Francis W. Little House II
Deephaven, Minnesota / demolished

William B. Greene House
Aurora, Illinois

1913

Harry S. Adams House
Oak Park, Illinois

1915

Ravine Bluffs Development Sculpture
Glencoe, Illinois

Edmund F. Brigham House
Glencoe, Illinois

Sherman M. Booth House
Glencoe, Illinois
Ravine Bluffs Development

Charles R. Perry House
Glencoe, Illinois
Ravine Bluffs Development

Hollis R. Root House
Glencoe, Illinois
Ravine Bluffs Development

William F. Kier House
Glencoe, Illinois
Ravine Bluffs Development

William F. Ross House
Glencoe, Illinois
Ravine Bluffs Development

Lute and Daniel Kissam House
Glencoe, Illinois
Ravine Bluffs Development

Emil Bach House
Chicago, Illinois

Arthur L. Richards Small House
Milwaukee, Wisconsin
American System-Built Homes

Arthur L. Richards Bungalow
Milwaukee, Wisconsin
American System-Built Homes

Lewis E. Burleigh House
Wilmette, Illinois
American System-Built Homes

1916

Frederick C. Bogk House
Milwaukee, Wisconsin

Ernest Vosburgh House
Grand Beach, Michigan

Joseph J. Bagley Cottage
Grand Beach, Michigan

W. S. Carr Cottage
Grand Beach, Michigan

Arthur R. Munkwitz Duplex Apartments
Milwaukee, Wisconsin
American System Ready-Cut

Arthur L. Richards Duplex Apartments
Milwaukee, Wisconsin
American System Ready-Cut

Henry J. Allen House
Wichita, Kansas

1917

Ida and Grace McElwain House
IdaLake Bluff, Illinois
American System-Built Homes

Stephen M. B. Hunt House II
Oshkosh, Wisconsin
American System-Built Homes

Guy C. Smith House
Chicago, Illinois
American System-Built Homes

H. H. Hyde House
Chicago, Illinois
American System-Built Homes

Oscar A. Johnson House
Evanston, Illinois
American System-Built Homes

Delbert W. Meier House
Monona, Iowa
American System-Built Homes

Wilbert Wynant House
Gary, Indiana
American System-Built Homes

Aisaku Hayashi House
Tokyo, Japan

1918

Arinobu Fukuhara House
Gora, Hakone, Japan

1920

Charles Heisen House
Villa Park, Illinois
American System-Built Homes

INDEX

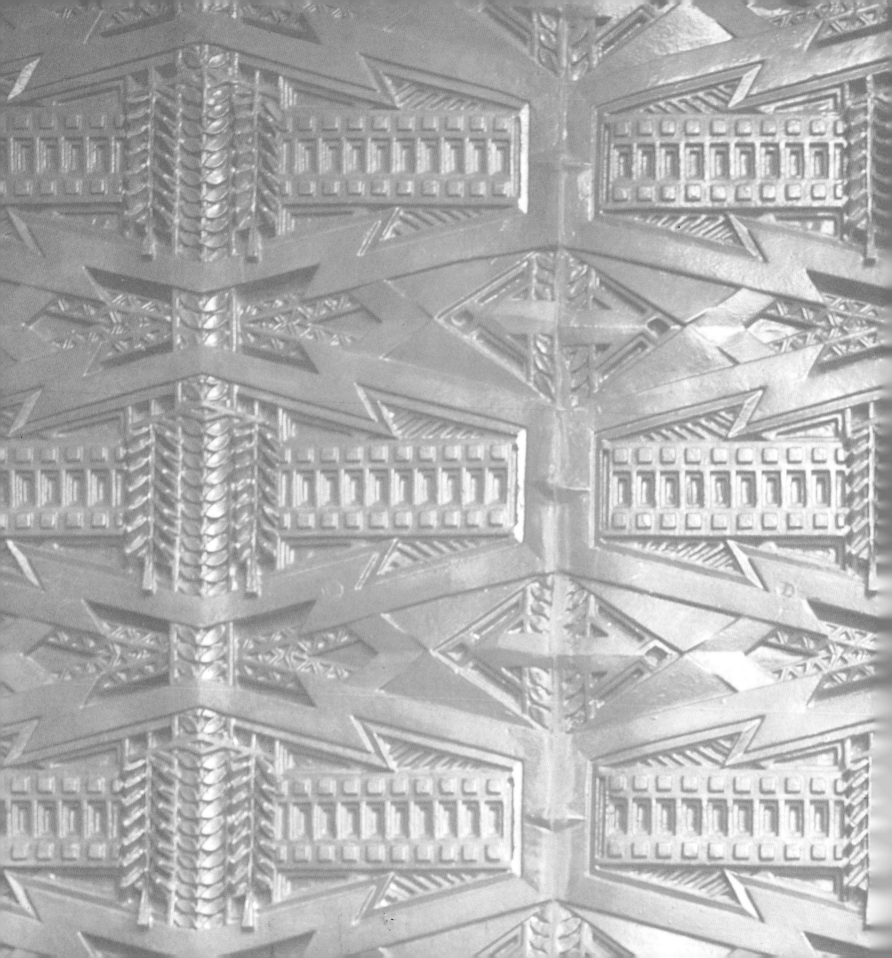